Sleeping Through the Night... and Other Lies

Sandi Kahn Shelton

Sleeping Through the Night
Copyright © 1999 by Sandi Kahn Shelton
ISBN-13: 978-1544072852
ISB-10:1544072856

NYLA Publishing
350 7th Avenue, Suite 2003, NY 10001, New York.
http://www.nyliterary.com

Dedication

To Benbo, Baba, and Stephos

Acknowledgments

So many people helped me write this book—Some by sharing stories of the outrageous things that were going on in their own households, and others by providing child care so I could get a chance to get the words entered into the computer.

First, I have unending gratitude to my editor, Jennifer Enderlin, and to my agent, Regula Noetzli, for treating this book like the small baby I knew it to be, and for encouraging me to write it.

And for the millions of funny stories, pieces of advice, and endless telephone conversations about kids, writing, and sleepless nights, I wish to thank Alice Mattison, Kay Kudlinski, Diane Cyr, Mary Squibb, Helen Myers, Joan Graham, Pat Shelton, Linda Shelton, Tracy Blanford, Jane Tamarkin, Bobbi Harshav, Deborah Hare, Karen Pritzker Vlock, Kate Flanagan, Kathy Parker, Roxanne Coady, Melissa Balmain, Jill Bergquist, Cathy Scherer, Barb Pavelko, Karen Bergantino, Debbie DeMusis, Caroline Rosenstone, Sari Bodi, Jennifer Smith, Alice Elliott Smith, my writing students at Southern Connecticut State University—and everyone who's ever been a member of the Children's Cooperative Day Care in New Haven.

Many thanks as well to the coffee shops who didn't mind when I, wild-eyed and trying to escape the ringing telephone in my house, plugged my laptop into their electrical outlets and sat for hours, drinking billions of cups of tea and writing. Thanks especially to Savvy Soda, Cilantro's, Anna's Temptations, Xando—and on occasion, the Dunkin' Donuts on Route 80.

And more thanks than I can ever express in words to my husband, Jim, who has been more than patient, especially on the day I dropped the laptop on the floor and panicked, and to my three amazing children, Benjamin, Allison, and Stephanie, who still insist they don't need any sleep.

Introduction

So You Went and Made a Baby—Now What?

So YOU DID IT. YOU WENT AND MADE YOURSELVES A BABY.

By now you've probably figured out how it happened. Oh sure, there was the sex. But you'd done that before without any babies getting started. This time, though, something mysterious and huge happened—egg and sperm actually introduced themselves to each other, shook hands, and then moved in together—and somehow all your vague ideas of someday have turned into right now.

Welcome to the Parent Club.

Perhaps you were sick of people saying, "So when are you guys going to have a kid, anyway?" Or maybe you suddenly noticed that when you were out in public, you could barely pay attention to what anybody was saying because you were so busy gazing at strangers' red-cheeked toddlers dozing in their strollers. And you couldn't help it; you'd stare at the parents, checking them out for signs of premature wear and tear, and find yourself relieved if it seemed they were still able to walk upright.

Or maybe—and this happens more than you'd think—pregnancy just sort of started on its own, as though the baby itself issued a policy statement: "Attention, People I Have Chosen As Parents: I have waited in the World of Ideas

1

for just about as long as I can stand. I will now be making an appearance on earth in approximately nine months. PS. I can make do with your spare room, but you'll have to get all that junk out of there. And by the way, we up here in the World of Ideas found it very amusing that you thought that diaphragm didn't have any holes in it."

However it happened, one day your time of childlessness simply ran out, and here you are: a couple with a kid.

On the one hand, you've probably realized that if the two of you can survive pregnancy and everyone's horror stories about childbirth, you can probably survive anything, even parenthood.

But then there's the other hand, that voice in your ear that's always too happy to remind you how incompetent you've always been in life. It's there to remind you how badly you did, in fact, with that stupid parenthood experiment in junior high, where you had to carry around a raw egg for a week without letting it drop—and how you went through ten eggs before you finally got the idea of hard-boiling the thing so it could survive to be two weeks old.

By now it's occurred to you that if you try to hard-boil the baby, the authorities will come. And that besides feeding it and keeping it moderately clean, there's not an equivalent thing you can do for a baby to make sure it lives. Or doesn't get hurt. Or makes it through seventh grade unscathed. Or even learns how to roll over.

To make matters worse, it seems that everywhere you turn, some expert or other is announcing that the first three years of life are so wildly important that a person's whole life, future earnings, and chances of going to the senior prom are all set in place during the precise time period when you, as parents, are as freaked out as you've ever been in your life. There's this nagging little feeling, supported, I'm afraid, by everyone from your parents to the federal government and the National Institutes of Health, that you could really Get It

2

Wrong and screw up the next generation royally. You, in fact, and your buddies who also may someday start procreating, could be personally responsible for the downfall of Western Civilization. Thanks to the way you've been living your life and are likely to be raising your child, human beings will most likely forget how to walk erect and simply turn into blobs, on their way, evolution-wise, toward being sea dwellers again.

But here's the truth: No one has ever felt remotely mentally healthy enough to raise a kid, and everybody gets it wrong every day. And even though the first three years are hair-raising and, yes, also extremely important, chances are your sense of goodwill—the same sense of goodwill that got you your life and your jobs and each other—can get you through. Remember this: Nobody—not even the head of the National Institute of Pediatric Health and Baby Management, if there were such a thing— knows what the hell to do when it's the middle of the night, and the kid is screaming and you've tried feeding, you've tried burping, you've tried walking, and you've tried changing diapers. You've even turned on the stereo, turned up the thermostat, turned down the thermostat, invented forty more verses to "I Found a Peanut," and now you're ready to consider alcoholic beverages all around, only the kid isn't twenty-one yet, and you're sure you'll get arrested.

Here are the crazy things people will tell you, and they are all true:

Sometimes turning on the clothes dryer works.

Sometimes walking very fast while singing the words to your high school fight song works.

Sometimes wrapping the baby's feet in a blanket helps.

Sometimes not eating garlic for a while will prevent other incidents like that, but probably not retroactively for this time.

But sometimes—I can't lie to you—you just have to stay up all night, holding onto this miserable little person, and all you can come away with is the knowledge that when the sun comes up, it doesn't get light all at once, but just kind of gradually gets lighter and lighter gray until you can start to notice things like flowers and lawn furniture and the individual leaves on the trees.

And that's when you realize the baby is asleep, and that you're most likely going to live through this time in your life.

Especially if you can laugh.

In fact, definitely if you can laugh.

Chapter 1: Babies and Other Critics

Home from the hospital

Coming home from the hospital is not at all like leaving for the hospital. For one thing, the one who actually gave birth no longer has to stop every few minutes to lean against the wall and say, "Hee hoo hee hoo," while the other searches through the bag to make sure there are enough tennis balls and sour lollipops, and to ask again what the hell tennis balls and sour lollipops have to do with having a baby in the first place.

All that is over. You have now brought the tennis balls and lollipops back home. (My opinion is that they were to let the hospital staff see if you're the submissive type who will bring absolutely anything they suggest that you pack. I'll bet no one even did so much as one volley with the balls.)

There's a sense of huge relief, walking in your front door again, bringing along the new family member you made. The main thing is that nine months of craziness is now officially over, and even though neither you nor your husband has any freaking idea what's about to happen to your lives, at least one thing is certain: Nobody is living inside of anybody else's body anymore. Everybody's responsible for taking in food and oxygen. And someday, you feel certain, you'll even be able to walk over to your closet and pick out something to wear that doesn't have a pregnancy bulge to it.

Many people think the Moment of Homecoming is a good time to go climb right into that bed you've missed and get your recovery well under way. Still other, more neurotic types would say this is an excellent time to turn on your workout tape and start flattening your stomach. It isn't.

This is a good time to start planning your strategy for living through the next few days.

The visitors are storming the gates

When you first bring a new baby home, it's unbelievable how many people are going to drop everything in their own lives and come to see it. People who wouldn't have gone to the trouble of crossing the street to say hello to you a few weeks ago are going to insist on "running by for a quick minute, just to get a look at the baby." There's something about a new member of the species that gets the whole planet in the mood to drive over to its house and get a bead on it.

Some of these people you will want to see, and some you will not. Some of them, in fact, will be your relatives, whom it is difficult to discourage and still maintain the kind of civility that will ensure tranquil holidays from now on.

The important thing to remember is that anyone who comes over should be willing to do some work before leaving. I know, I know. You might not be the type who wants your old elementary school chums taking out the trash for you—but think of this: It gives them a sense of purpose while they're visiting, and it keeps you from having to lug your postpartum selves to the garbage can later.

Putting visitors to work is a very tricky proposition, but it can be managed. The important thing to remember is that the new parents—that's you guys—are exhausted and deserve all the help you can get. After all, you just went through hours and hours of labor together, not to mention the nine-month construction project you've been involved in.

Besides that, at least one of you is probably lactating. And your hormones are rampaging. You need to lie in bed and gaze at your baby, and if other people want to be there watching you do that, they should be doing two things: agreeing with you wholeheartedly that this is the All-Time Most Adorable Baby There Ever Was, and then, when they are done with this agreeing, they should be fixing you some dinner, or at least a nice glass of lemonade.

You will know that things are going very badly indeed if you find yourself in the kitchen serving the guests. Do not let this happen. If you find yourself with a tray in your hands, what works every time is to double over suddenly, closing your eyes for just a second. Everyone will remember that you are in a delicate condition, and they—if they are any kind of friends at all—will insist you go back to bed while they take over the refreshment portion of the visit.

Worst of all, though, is if you are in the kitchen, fixing them some tea, and they are telling you that your child seems to have an odd little point to his head. That, I would think, would be grounds for immediate eviction.

Even when things are going swell, it's good to have a plan to clear the room, if you should suddenly get sick of everybody and want to be alone with your baby. I have found that launching into a description of the birth process itself will normally scare away any men, elderly people, and childless women who might be visiting, especially if you use a few key phrases, like, "bloody show," "mucous plug," or "meconium in the amniotic fluid." This method generally won't work with women who have had babies themselves; indeed, such teasing details will probably launch them into a Gruesome Birth Stories Competition.

Fortunately, there's something that works even better with women who've had children. All you have to do is whisper, "I'm soooo tired," and they'll most likely take it upon themselves in the name of sisterhood to clear the room on your behalf. Women forever after remember the kind of

7

tiredness that comes after they've pushed a seven-pound object out of their body, and they won't be the ones to suggest that maybe you could get up and spiff the place up a little, and while you're at it, put on a pot of tea.

Take advantage of this situation while you can. And when the guests are getting their coats and leaving, it doesn't hurt to smile sweetly and ask if they wouldn't mind taking a bag or two of garbage on their way out.

If you can't say cheese, at least you can run

Unbelievable as it may seem, some people aren't coming to visit you. It may seem as though everyone you've ever spoken to or passed in the grocery store is there, but in fact, some people in your life can't, due to circumstances beyond their control, make it to your house.

They are on the telephone begging you for photographs.

It is safe to say that never again in your life will there be so much need for photographs—starting on day one. Here you are, leaking from most of your orifices and suddenly in charge of a hairless creature that looks as though it could start throwing its weight around at any moment, and your relatives are claiming that every hideous moment you're going through must be documented photographically. Someday, if the world keeps going the way it is and classes are held on every subject imaginable, Lamaze instructors will hold a separate eight-week session on How to Take Great Baby Photos, and home-care agencies will send out photographers along with visiting nurses.

Face this fact right now: Friends and relatives are going to expect all kinds of photographic records coming from your household in a practically continuous stream. You will never be able to keep up with the demand. It's best if you accept right from the beginning that you can't do it and that you develop a thick skin when all your relatives are screaming at you.

I myself have a Postal Disorder, meaning that I can't ever seem to get things to the post office in any kind of timely manner whatsoever. And, as we all know, getting pictures to relatives is lots more complicated than simply getting to the post office; first there is the film-buying project, then the taking of the photos, then taking the film in to get developed, then picking it up, then getting copies made, writing the little notes, finding the address book, writing out the envelopes—and only then do you get to the post office part, which by then anyone would be too exhausted to think of.

In our house, we have pictures of all three of the children coming home from the hospital for the first time, and I have to confess to you now: Not one of these pictures was from the Actual Homecoming.

I'm afraid they were all staged reenactments, some as many as three or four days later, or perhaps even weeks later, who knows? We took the damn picture whenever it happened that we could both locate the camera and manage to have at least two of us in dry, clean clothing that didn't have some kind of digested or undigested milk on it. At least we got to it before it was time to take the First Day of Kindergarten picture, and sometimes that's all that a person can ask of herself. (A hint, though: If the baby has lost that identifiable newborn scrawniness or is, say, able to walk, you should take the Hospital Homecoming picture from a very great distance.)

I find it helps if you do manage to take the Standard Baby Photos That Show That You Really Did Come Up With an Actual Kid. There are some pictures that simply must be taken, or your friends and relatives will have a tough time forgiving you, and you'll be forever spending Thanksgiving dinners with them trying to justify your lapse in competence. These are almost *de rigueur:*

- Coming through the front door for what you will forever after claim was the first time.
- The first bath.
- The moment after the first bath, when the towel was draped adorably over the baby's head. (This is to prove that all three of you made it through the bath.)
- The baby swinging in the baby swing. (Keep in mind that newborns in a baby swing often look as though their necks are broken, and you don't want your relatives calling to yell at you about infant posture, so you'll have to prop the baby in a pseudo-upright position and then snap the picture within the first five seconds before he slumps down again.)
- The baby screaming. (Don't ask me why people want this; I think it might be because it proves that you really did have a real, genuine baby and aren't just posing with some plastic doll or something. Surely you've noticed that dolls are never posed in the screaming position.)
- The baby sleeping—preferably on the father's chest.
- The baby nursing. (This is one of those keepsake pictures that for years will make everyone, including you, say, "Ahhhh," at the sight of the baby's round little head nestled so softly against the mountain of your breast. Some things to keep in mind in taking this picture: Make sure it's not at the moment of the milk letting down, when you're liable to be gritting your teeth and saying "Yikes!" instead of looking like the radiant Madonna you wish to portray. The facial expression that accompanies the word "Yikes!" is probably not something you want in the baby book for years to come.)

You will doubtlessly come up with many more pictures that beg to be taken; I've only attempted to mention the time-honored classics. But let me caution you that there are some pictures you must never take, at the risk of alienating your spouse, big-time.

Pictures You Must Never Ever Take

- Pictures in which either adult of the household is crying.
- Artistic "mood" photos that show dirty dishes, screaming baby, half-opened bathrobe, and despairing expressions.
- Those that show illegal activities, such as letting the baby ride in your arms in the car instead of in the car seat.
- The ones in which stretch marks, eye bags, or sagging bellies figure prominently.
- The baby's face being licked by the dog.
- The baby licking the dog's face.

I once personally engineered a merger, you know

Like any other new skill you're learning, parenthood takes some practice. And there are going to be some mistakes. Not really horrible mistakes, certainly, but things you definitely will want to improve upon as you go along. For instance, once I was very industriously bathing my two-week-old baby in the kitchen sink. So intent was I on making sure I was truly cleaning off all the various poopish areas that I didn't realize, until I heard the sputter, that I had her turned upside down—and the top of her head was submerged in the water. This, I could see right away, was not an award-winning bath experience. The Mother of the Year people would have crossed my name right off the list, I'm sure.

This is the kind of thing I'm talking about. No great harm was done; she didn't even turn out to be afraid of the water later in life. But still, we both had to go sit down for a long time after that incident. I don't know about her, but my legs were definitely made of rubber, and I had to work really hard to think of a good excuse to explain to her why that happened.

You see, I think it's important that the baby thinks that you know what you're doing. For a while, you may have to fake this, although I have always been afraid that, because they live so much on the sensory level, babies will pick up any vibe of fakery I might put out. (This is mainly because I lived in California when my first baby was born. By the time I had the other two in Connecticut, years later, it had fortunately become illegal to use the words *sensory level* and *vibe* in the same sentence, so I didn't worry about that anymore.)

Anyhow, I think it's a good plan to start in right away telling the baby all the things you've accomplished in your life. They don't care a great deal about mergers and real estate transactions just yet, but they pick up on the note of pride in your voice, and I think when they're out with the other babies in the strollers they can hold their heads high. Assuming they're at that physical stage, of course.

I have even been known to make little speeches. "You may think that because I got the diaper on backwards that first day that I'm some sort of incompetent wuss," I once told a skeptical baby. "But I want you to know that I have been on this planet so long that I can remember when diapers didn't even have tapes. In the old days, if someone did a diaper the wrong way, chances were good that someone was going to get stuck with a pin, probably either you or me. At least with tapes there are no lacerations."

A baby will be awed by this kind of information. I also found it helpful at times to address their fears directly. "I know there were a few bad moments with that bath the other day when you were thinking you might go right under the water," you might say. "But really, it was my first offense. I've been taking baths myself for decades without any ill consequences, and I'm sure we'll manage just fine from now on. By the way, did you know that I can type ninety-five words a minute, and I once single-handedly changed a tire on the highway?"

A day may come when it seems your credibility is particularly low. At that time, point out that you are the one who knows where the food comes from—particularly if it's true that your own body is so intelligent it happens to be making it on demand. I mean, this is an amazing feat right in itself, and the baby should be impressed as hell by this. I have had to explain on occasion to the baby that I was as surprised as he was that my body had this particular talent. "Before you came along, these were just ornamental, and now just look at how competent they are!"

I have several friends who believe that they got babies who slept through the night before most other people's babies did simply because they spoke with such authority on the need for sleep.

My friend Jennifer denies this now, but I clearly remember her saying to me when her first child was six months old: "I simply showed the baby that I was the resident sleep authority, and that I happened to know that humans slept when it was dark and got up when it was light, and that was that. No discussion."

The fates took swift revenge on such a statement, and subsequently sent Jennifer two babies who didn't buy that whole sleep authority stuff. They exposed her for what she really was all along with that first child: merely lucky.

If you should happen to have been issued one of the babies who is a child prodigy when it comes to sleeping through the night, then I think it would be best all around if you didn't brag about it to other people. Not that you would ever brag, of course, but there is a temptation to think that such good fortune might have been due to something wonderful you did. But believe me, if you mention this too loudly in public, you'll end up with a kid who isn't fully toilet trained until he's a freshman in high school.

The name game

One of the main things you'll find yourself doing during the first few days is thinking about the baby's name. Okay, regretting the baby's name. It's such a huge responsibility having to give this person the name she'll be stuck with for the rest of her life, and if you have any tendency at all toward brooding, you can hardly find a better topic to brood over than why you caved in to pressure and chose that particular name. Even if you thought you loved it, you'll find that just the act of saying it over and over again the first few days makes you think you might hate it after all.

I have hardly met any postpartum person who wasn't determined to go to the courthouse as soon as possible and do whatever was necessary to get a new name for the kid, even if she'd been calling the baby his potential new name all through fetus-hood. This is because you look down at this scrawny, red-faced little person and you can't imagine that he'll ever grow into being a Herbert Francis III, which you've just declared him to be. You've obviously turned your child into some kind of joke.

The truth is that some names just look ridiculous on new babies. They obviously belong to people from another generation. This is why nicknames happen. You should rest assured that whatever name you have chosen, other people are going to take over and call your kid something else altogether: Goober or Corky or Stretch, or something like that.

You'd like to take a few days to get to know the baby before saddling it with a name. But the hospital can't deal with that. Soon after you've given birth, the nurse comes in with that little form and asks for the name. If you have no idea, you feel just the tiniest bit like an idiot. As though you missed the introductions in the delivery room or something.

You feel like saying, "I'm sorry, there was so much going on that I didn't quite catch the name. If you'd just go into the nursery and ask him, I'd be so grateful."

There's a lot of pressure, no doubt about it. When the nurse came in to accost my friend Leslie and get a name for the baby, Leslie said the only name in the whole world she could ever remember hearing was Hermione. All the other names had been mysteriously erased from her brain tapes, as though she were in an episode from *The Twilight Zone* or something. Hospitals have that effect on some people. She was about to cave in and just name the baby Hermione, come what may, when her husband happened to show up. He had a few brain cells intact, enough to remember that they both liked the name Andrea, and so they did not have to go to the courthouse the next week and get things put right.

When I was in the hospital, having had my first child, my husband and I couldn't think of a single name for him. The name we'd been calling him throughout the pregnancy had suddenly soured on me after nine months of saying it to everyone. I was sitting in bed one day, reading the baby name book and worrying that the hospital staff wasn't going to let me go home until I picked out something, when the nurse's aide said she had the perfect name for me.

"It's the name I picked for my son, and I've never been sorry," she said.

I picked up the pen, ready to write.

"Socrates Euphrates," she said proudly.

I picked up the baby name book again. I'd made it as far as the Bs, and suddenly the name Benjamin looked absolutely wonderful. It was the most beautiful name in the world, and why hadn't I realized this before?

"Benjamin!" I told his father. "Let's call him Benjamin!"

All our friends and family agreed this was a splendid decision—which is a rarity indeed. It was the Name That Had Everything: style, heft, even a decent nickname.

Three weeks later, at the Lamaze class reunion, I discovered that six baby boys had been born. They were all named Benjamin. The four girls were Jennifer.

Things Everyone Now Expects You to Know How to Do

- Take professional-quality pictures of the baby and actually mail them out to people.
- Be able to put together a crib that arrived in forty-five thousand pieces, using a diagram written in Portuguese.
- Explain to others what the baby is trying to convey when she's crying.
- Divine whether the kid is going to need a hat and heavy blanket by the end of any given day—and remember to pack it, along with everything else that might be needed.
- Change the baby's diaper in a crowded restaurant without anyone guessing what you're doing.
- Put a sleeping baby in a snowsuit, then in the car seat, then in the Snugli, then do the grocery shopping, load up the car with at least a week's worth of food, take the baby out of the Snugli and back into the car seat, and then back home, where—presto!—you remove the still-sleeping baby from the snowsuit and put her in the crib.
- Come up with a good reason why you didn't name the baby after Great Uncle Aloysius, whose only wish in life was that he be remembered that way.

A new mother's role: The human snack bar

This is as good a time as any to talk about the fact that your body now has learned some new tricks, fluid-wise. Nothing it has learned, though, is more amazing than the fact that it now manufactures a food substance. You, in fact, are the equivalent of a small factory.

There are days you feel like an ordinary house cow, if there is such a thing. For the first few days it seems that if a baby cries anywhere on the planet, immediately your own personal breasts rush to produce gallons of milk to fill it up with. It doesn't even have to be your baby; your body has seemingly decided that it will take on the plight of anyone under the age of a year old who might be hungry. You are in touch, as they say, with your bovine tendencies.

In between becoming so altruistic as to want to feed everyone in sight, your breasts leak, drip, grow rock-hard, tingle, and enthusiastically spurt milk whenever possible. In fact, often just to go in public, you have to wear garments that resemble plastic cups or sanitary napkins to disguise the fact that you are making the most of your mammalian heritage.

But even with all the hassles and clothing-soaking, it's worth it to be a human snack bar, and I can tell you why in five little words: the middle of the night.

Babies tend to think the middle of the night is one of the great times to eat, which is something that distinguishes them from most other people on earth, who take tremendous pleasure in getting uninterrupted sleep specifically during those hours. I was never very competent in the wee hours, particularly when it involved hearing loud screeching noises next to my ear. That may be just me. I've had friends who said it didn't bother them a bit to wake up, hearing their baby crying, and then make their way down to the kitchen, where they needed to (1) open a can of formula, (2) find a clean bottle and nipple, (3) find a pot, (4) fill it with water, (5) heat up the bottle for about three minutes, (6) test the formula to make sure it was not too hot or too cold, and then (7) sit down somewhere, in an upright position, while the baby—finally not screaming anymore—ate until it dropped off to sleep again. Some of these people even admitted that while the formula was heating up on the stove, they took the opportunity to wrestle the now apoplectically shrieking baby down onto the changing table, and actually change the diaper.

Now, you see, there is none of that with nursing. Instead, the scenario goes like this: The baby starts to whimper in the night, you go get it, plug it into the breast outlet which is conveniently located on the front of you, and everybody goes immediately back to sleep. Even if you're one of those who doesn't want to put the baby in the bed next to you, you still have eliminated the entire trip to the kitchen and the major screaming fit that tends to make the neighbors so surly toward you the next day.

I loved nursing for many reasons, not the least of which was it meant I didn't have to wash any bottles. Nor did I have to make any mad-dash trips to the store at all hours, suddenly remembering that we were down to two drops of formula, only to discover that the store was also out of it, and I was going to have to drive aimlessly around looking for a store with a better distribution system.

With nursing, I was never out of my brand. Sometimes, if I ate something funky, the baby would start to taste it and then pull away and stare at me like, "What the hell is this broccoli with garlic sauce doing mixed in with the main course?"

But then the baby would go back to sucking away and, just like always, we'd both fall sound asleep. It was, I realized, like having one of those hotel wet bars right in the bedroom.

Actual Known Advantages to Having an Infant— For Those Days When You Can't Remember

- There's some kind of tax deduction you'll now get.
- Whenever anybody asks you to do something you'd rather not do, you can always say that the baby is sick.

- If you're still wearing your bathrobe at four in the afternoon and you've just polished off a whole box of Ding Dongs, no one will ask you why you're not more together.
- Babies, unlike other people, are always happy to see you whenever you come into view.
- For a good long time, you don't have to hold your stomach in.
- Their toys are fun to play with.
- Sometimes, watching them sleep in your arms, you feel a rush of tenderness so great that it's as if your heart has just opened up four more ratchets.

Decide right now what you're going to call it

One way your life is about to change dramatically is that you're going to be talking about excrement nearly all the time. And here's the real shocker: It will even seem interesting to you. There will be days when you call up your spouse simply to report on the size, color, consistency, and interval between bowel movements, and your spouse will react with exactly the same fascination as if you'd called to describe the Jaguar you'd just bought. It's yet another thing that gives you the sense that the two of you have your own private landscape in this World of Babies.

But in order to do this, the two of you have to know what you're going to call it. I know you're busy, but I think coming up with a name for it has to be one of your more immediate tasks. You don't want to get stuck needing to come up with a word sometime when you are out there in public, with a two-year-old you're trying to potty train. At a time like that, believe me, the only word you'll be able to remember is shit, and you won't like how it sounds when you're crooning, "Come on, darling, let's shit in the potty."

And not that you want to cave in to peer pressure, but shit has some other drawbacks too. Strangers will give you horrified looks when your little one screeches it, which all little ones do at one time or another. It's bad enough if he's yelling it because he recognizes it as a perfectly wonderful swearword, guaranteed to get a reaction; but you're likely to feel really rotten if he's using it correctly.

The only thing that shit has going for it is that it is anything but cutesy. You don't want to do cutesy when it comes to the bathroom department. You've probably not called it duty or doo-doo or even poo-poo for many years now, and I say, why revert back to those days when there are so many other good words out there?

No, the word of the moment is poop. There are many good reasons to go with this, mainly that it has a cartoonish, lighthearted feel to it, so that even at those times (much later, of course) when you and the kid are discussing it loudly and publicly, you know strangers won't be shocked by your word of choice. They may be flabbergasted that you are engaged in such a bizarre conversation out in the world, but at least when the word poop is hurled through the air, they'll know several things about you right off: One is that you are on the cutting edge of parenthood, and that you have taken some trouble to find the best word. The other is that you are not a cutesy type, and that while you're not so earthy as to go for the more disconcerting shit, you also don't go in for the kind of 1950s euphemisms that might cause other people to wince.

A friend of mine used bowel movement, interspersed with B.M., but ultimately, her friends decided she sounded too arch saying those things. It made us all reflect on the fact that she had a big-deal law degree and tended toward a certain stuffiness in her personal life.

Somebody else I know used to say constantly to her child, "Do you have to go number two?" I've often wondered how he later felt about the subject of arithmetic, knowing that one number has to be associated at all times with a bodily function. I think this could create a certain confusion later on that so easily could be avoided.

No, I think it's safe to say that the best choice for today is poop.

And while we're at it, the other is pee.

You may not have the right to sing the blues, but why let that stop you?

"Hormones."

That is the correct answer to almost any question a new mother is asked for the first few weeks.

Why are you crying? Why is there milk leaking out all over the front of you? Why are you really crying? Why is your hair coming out in clumps? No, what's really, really going on with you?

It's all hormones, I'm afraid. Even if you are undeniably the happiest and most relieved you've ever been in your whole miserable life, with a baby at last, and by God, it even has ten fingers and toes, not to mention the right number of eyes, noses, and mouths—even if everything went better than you could have ever asked for in your wildest crazy dreams, there still is a moment when you will be sitting in front of the television set, and a commercial will come on, advertising something like long distance rates, and who knows what it will set off in you: the sudden realization that life on this planet is transient and ephemeral, the certainty that your baby is going to be as disgusted with you in twenty years as you are with your parents, or even a wild sense of regret that you didn't make out with Bobby Sullivan back in seventh grade when you were playing Spin the Bottle. But anyway, there you are, sobbing on the couch, pounding your fists, and blubbering as though the end of the world has come.

Men, sad to say, probably can't use the hormones excuse. If they are walking into walls and staring out into space, they have to think up some other possible explanation. Not getting enough sleep is the most socially acceptable excuse, because it just won't do to blubber to the boss, "I just can't take it that our poor little baby is someday going to have to go to eighth grade!"

For me, it was McDonald's that pushed me right off the emotional ledge. Right after I brought the baby home from the hospital, McDonald's started running an ad about a little boy and his dog who were separated for a whole day while the kid was in school, and then—this can still make me get all teary—the school bus came home and the two were reunited, with the most joyous face-licking and grinning you ever saw.

I tell you, I would get hysterical every time, while my wide-eyed husband sat nervously, with his fingers poised by the 911 button, ready to call in the authorities at a moment's notice. It was pretty obvious he hadn't read all the books about pregnancy and childbirth I'd been thrusting at him since the day we did the at-home pregnancy test, or he would have known all about the routine symptoms of postpartum blues.

I'd have to sit there, gasping through my sobs. "This is all— perf-perfectly normal behavior," I'd say. "I'm sup-sup-supposed to be acting this way." Then the look on his face would make me burst out laughing, but just as he was joining me in a relieved belly laugh, I'd remember the little boy and his dog again, and I'd dissolve back into tears.

"Yeah, right," he'd say. "Everyone acts this way. Just let me know when you want the ambulance."

It was tough to explain how, even though I adored the baby and was so glad not to be pregnant anymore, I simply couldn't stop crying. One night, thinking it was that I was trying to do too much, household-wise, my husband went out to buy us hamburgers from Wendy's for dinner. It was about a million degrees, too hot even to go near the kitchen anyway. I gave him my very precise hamburger order: meat, lettuce, tomatoes, no pickles, no onions, no sauce. And French fries. And a Coke, lots of ice.

When he came home, he handed me a hamburger laden with lots of pickles, onions, and sauce. The fries were cold, the Coke wasn't.

Naturally I cried. In fact, I wept so bitterly that he kept saying, "What is it? What is it? This just can't be the fact that Wendy's made your hamburger wrong."

All I could say was, "Can't you see what's happening? The people at Wendy's don't care about anybody but themselves. They're terrible, awful people who shouldn't be allowed to be around other people's food. The whole world is just made up of the most terrible people, and now we're bringing a poor little child into the world, and I can't even imagine the hamburgers he'll have to eat in his lifetime, all the junk that unfeeling people will put on them—"

My husband stared at me. Then he said, "This is really hormones, isn't it?"

I said, "Yes."

"So, probably even if the hamburger had been made perfectly, you'd still be in tears?"

"Oh, sure, go ahead and start insulting me, the mother of your child, buddy boy!"

Since you're already not sleeping...

I have to break some rather bad news to you, so I will try to do it gently. Many people—even people who came to see you and the baby—are going to expect a formal birth announcement from you. This is a vile custom that must have gotten started back when households had wet nurses, upstairs maids, and full-time chefs. Even worse is that people feel cheated if you don't include a charming little note, mentioning how delighted you and your husband are to be parents, along with some brief statement of the baby's accomplishments. (Since this is presumably being written in the first weeks of life, you may have to search hard to find something. "Little Johnny burped three times yesterday, during his two P.M. feeding alone" will do in a pinch.)

The best birth announcements include an hours-old picture of the baby, but this, I think, is above and beyond what most people can manage without a devoted staff.

The birth announcements I have sent out have mostly arrived well before the baby's first birthday and contained many telltale stains of milk (both spit-up and fresh), fingerprints, tea, sweat, and tears. I feel this, more than a general description, provided people with a real feeling for what we were going through. You don't want to mislead people into thinking parenthood is just a walk in the park.

One more thing: After they get the announcement, they will send you a present. And then you need to write them a thank-you note, telling even more accomplishments. By then, a worthy accomplishment may be that you slept four hours at a stretch one day.

Babies: The ultimate birth control devices

I hate to bring this up, but one of you is sure to start brooding about it soon, so I might as well go ahead and mention it.

Sex.

Remember sex? You may have once thought you couldn't live without it, but it's amazing how, when you're getting up to forty-five minutes of sleep at night, you hardly ever even think of it anymore, particularly if you're the woman in the equation. Plus, there are all these other little factors involved in helping you forget about the joys of union: The main one is that you're constantly united with that eight-pounder who's hanging on your breasts most of the time. Then there are the stretch marks that you imagine make you look like an army vehicle has made tracks across your mid-regions—which is not to overlook the fact that your ya-ya already has enough complaints of its own.

You hardly feel like putting on the soft music, lighting the candles, and getting down to a serious snuggle— even if you *did* manage to give the baby the slip for a half hour or so.

But, cheer up: You will again. Look around you at all the people who have multiple numbers of children; they didn't just have sex to get the first one and then buy the others at the store, you know. Amazingly enough, you have to have sex again and again, if you want more than one child.

My friend Sarah once had this discussion with her ten-year-old son, who was marveling at the fact that their male cat had managed to get both of their female cats pregnant at the same time. Yes, it was a touchy subject, but they were doing fine with it until Jeff said he couldn't believe something like that could ever happen in the world.

"But, Jeff," Sarah said, "you know how babies get made, don't you? You do know about sex, right?"

"Well, sure," he said, "I know all about sex. But twice it can happen?"

The good news is that it does happen twice, even in one lifetime. Maybe not today, maybe not tomorrow—but someday soon you're going to want to have some again.

You belong in the movies

Despite the fact that you're weeping a lot of the time, and you've also got some heavy what-to-call-it decisions to make, this is the best time in your whole life to go to the movies. I don't know why this isn't a better-advertised fact— movie theaters themselves should include New Baby Specials, I think. Yet in all the child-rearing books I've read, not one of them mentions that all parents of newborns should be taking them to theaters.

Why? I think the reason should be obvious. You need to get out of the house, yet you also need to sit down a lot. And the theater is dark. You can even work out some of your postpartum depression stuff if you pick a sad movie. No one will wonder why you're crying. You won't have to look over at your husband and remind him again about the hormone thing you're going through.

The best part is that the baby likes it. It's loud and it's dark in the theater, and newborns just settle down in your lap and pretend it's still the Good Old Days, back before they were born and there were so many bright lights to contend with. Wrap them up tight, lift up your shirt, and the baby can nurse and sleep for the entire evening—and you can cry and laugh and yet still be having a date with your husband. You are, in fact, tending to your marriage.

Believe me, the day is coming when you can't take this individual anywhere where silence is required (now I am talking about the baby), so you might as well enjoy it while you can. It may be your last chance to see first-run movies without having to pay the exorbitant prices baby-sitters get these days. And even then—even if you've made the decision to hire a registered nurse who successfully raised nine children of her own—you'll still worry about how the baby's doing at home the whole time you're gone.

No, you can get away with this going to the movies caper for quite a little while, if you manage it right. And don't worry; you'll know when the time comes to quit. For us, it happened when the baby was about six months old, and we'd gone to a downtown theater to see a movie about John Lennon. Somebody was having a conversation in the theater during the previews of the coming attractions, and a guy in the next row stood up and threw his Coke at the person doing the talking. "I like my movies QUIET!" he screamed, in quite a persuasive way.

We decided right then we couldn't guarantee him the quiet he might require, especially with our very wide-awake baby who had just developed the very adorable skill of making raspberries.

"I'm remembering I don't like John Lennon so very much," I whispered to my husband, and before we had to field a Coke coming over to land on our heads, just for saying that, we got up and crept out silently.

The kid made raspberries all the way home, in between performing her other new talent of the moment, saying, "Bobobobobobobobo."

Until your kids can do a raspberry, though, I think you're going to do just fine. And after that—well, you'll stay home a lot and make raspberries together.

Signs That Things Are Pretty Much Normal at Your House

- You've now learned to sleep with your hand hanging into the bassinet, keeping the pacifier plugged into the baby's mouth through the night.
- You can't even remember which side you last nursed on, so one of your breasts seems to be ballooning and the other looks like a used tube of toothpaste.
- There's a deep path worn into the carpet around the dining room table where you've walked the baby through the dinner hour every day for months.
- All your clothes have white, stiff stuff on the shoulders— and that looks perfectly acceptable to you now.
- The happiest you've ever been in your life was when the baby fell asleep in your arms and seemed to have a smile on her face.
- At least one of your childless friends has had to remind you that baby diarrhea is not a good topic at the dinner table.

Chapter 2 :
Things You Might Not Have Thought Of

The fun of parenthood lingo

Your baby will hardly be dried off after birth before people start using bizarre words in your presence. These, you might as well know, are the technical terms of parenthood, and, as in the case of any jargon that comes with a new job, you will look like a fool if you keep having to ask what they mean.

I know these aren't words you ever wanted to know the meanings of. If you are a person of any dignity at all, you were most likely not looking forward to the day when you could publicly chat with your friends about "onesies," those one-piece baby stretch garments that snap in the crotch. But chances are, that's what is in store for you just the same. You have to get used to people—particularly salespeople and overzealous gift-buyers—wanting to know how many onesies you have managed to collect. My friend Bob once sneered, "Not only do we not have any onesies, but we're starting to run low on twosies and threesies."

This is the kind of attitude that you want to avoid, if possible. There are enough irritating things people are going to say to you now that you're a parent that it doesn't pay to waste a perfectly good fit of snippiness on lingo. Besides, I guarantee you, these are words you will hear dozens of times each day for the first few months—and then you'll never hear anybody refer to them again until you get another baby.

Here, then, are some words parents will throw around, and that you might want to throw right back at them.

Zwieback: A perfectly dreadful piece of toast that you buy in a box. It was obviously toasted sometime near the beginning of the last century and since that time has been calcifying until it's now approximately equivalent to diamonds in terms of hardness. When it gets so hard that it no longer resembles anything edible, it is sold—mostly to parents of infants.

What in the world does this substance have to do with babies? Although it was probably first developed as a primitive weapon system, since the ending of the Cold War its only known use is as a teething aid for babies. An additional benefit can be the powerful paste that infants produce from the wetted-down crumbs, more adhesive than any superglue on the market.

Colic: When your baby screams for no discernible reason, you get to call it colic. Most likely your baby is actually pondering the existential crisis of converting to an out-of-womb existence, but "colic" sounds better. Besides, this is one of those terms that people invented just so they wouldn't have to say over and over again, "I have no freaking idea why the baby won't stop crying, so stop asking me before I kill you." If, instead, you say, "Oh, it's colic," people will not only stop giving you an evil look as though you are the one responsible for making this perfectly innocent little person so miserable, but they will actually start to sympathize with you, which is exactly how it should be. Colic technically only lasts for the first few months and probably has something to do with the development of immature intestines, but many parents find they don't want to give it up as an excuse for that incessant, loathsome crying. One friend of mine insists that her high-school-age daughter still is very colicky, and I'm not going to be the one to argue with her.

Receiving Blankets: Until I had a baby, I thought that blankets only came in a few kinds: king-sized, full, twin, and possibly wool. Then people started sending me things they called receiving blankets, which were pieces of flannel approximately the size of pillowcases. My mother told me I was supposed to wrap up the baby in them—swaddle, I believe, is the real term for this—but since my babies were all born in the late spring and summer when it was mostly over 90 degrees, they weren't interested in this form of mothering. Receiving blankets, I think, are blankets you receive from other people. Don't make the mistake of buying them. Then, I suppose, they would be called purchasing blankets.

Binky: This is not a word you ever want to hear yourself saying, I know, but it can be useful to know its meaning so that when other people ask about the location of the binky, you won't be standing there blinking in astonishment. The binky is, for some unknown reason, the pacifier. Probably the first person to coin this term was eighteen months old, but somehow we got stuck with it in our regular English language, and now parents everywhere can be heard asking where the goddamned binky has gotten to. I want you to know that I have had three children and have yet to utter this word out loud. (This is a fact I'm considering including on my resume.)

Cradle Cap: This sounds delightful, like something with lace and maybe even a silk ribbon tied under the chin, but in fact it's a medical term for the crud that seems to grow on your baby's scalp. I'm convinced that this yucky substance is there only to make you feel like an inadequate parent—sort of Nature's way of pointing out that it doesn't matter how clean you try to keep the baby, there's always some substance glomming onto it that you can't quite get off. Someone told me once to wash the baby's hair in baby oil, but surely that way lies madness. Babies getting their hair washed are in a precarious enough spot without having the bath be in oil.

Umbilical Stump: I know that you are probably a perfectly nice person who wants to do absolutely the right thing for your baby, and I am sorry to be hitting you with good news and bad news all at once. But, really, you should know that that big black thing on the belly button is one day going to fall off—that's the good news part—and then you—you!—are going to have to decide what to do with it. Some people are squeamish about these things and don't want umbilical stumps hanging around the house, and so what if it took nine months to grow such a thing, and it is the physical manifestation of the deep mother-child bond? They have no problem at all tossing it in the trash can. In our house, though, we are all the worst kind of wimps, and so we have three umbilical stumps in a box, along with all the lost baby teeth. The box has a sign on it: Things That Fell Off the Children, and although we haven't yet gotten to the point of including warts and scabs, I wouldn't be surprised by anything I see in that box.

Prickly Heat: This is a rash that means the baby is too hot. It is different from the other rashes babies get, such as diaper rashes, basically because of location, and also because prickly heat doesn't get the press that diaper rash gets. There are even television and radio commercials for diaper rash remedies—but what if your child is afflicted with prickly heat? You don't get any information at all. The word prickly, I think, refers mostly to their personality when they have this rash.

Projectile Vomiting: I really hated to include this one, but everybody around you is going to mention it anyway, so you might as well hear it from me. Projectile vomiting is when the baby throws up so hard that instead of politely dribbling down the chin like most spit-up, it careens through your living room, down the hall, and through the bedroom windows, landing somewhere three towns away on an unsuspecting passerby who would probably sue you if only he knew where this was coming from. Whenever you mention to anyone that your baby spits up a lot (which they all do), if that person is like my mother, she will say, "Oh, my God, is it projectile vomiting?" Pediatricians like to hear about it if the vomit achieves a velocity of, say, fifty miles per hour.

Pablum: This is gray cereal matter that people will try to get you to feed the baby. When you buy it in the box, it resembles sand, and it tastes something like sand, also. Somehow, it has been determined to be the best starter food for babies, possibly because of its dust-like texture and the fact that it has virtually no taste. For some reason, food manufacturers think that tasting something delicious would be very bad for babies. Perhaps they picture a gang of infants going on strike and demanding better-tasting food before they will agree to learn to walk and talk. The best thing that can be said for pablum is that because of its neutral color, it blends in with most decor and carpeting. Just be glad somebody didn't decide that a kid's first food should be strained beets.

Soft Spot: If you're like most new parents, you will be hysterical at the idea of the soft spot. That's the place on the baby's head where the bones didn't grow together yet, another one of Nature's development *faux pas.* How much trouble, I ask you, would it have been for Nature to finish up with the head-bone building before pushing the baby out into the world? I mean, this thing actually pulses. You will spend many hours of the day and night worrying that you might somehow puncture it. I once called the pediatrician, weeping, because I had gotten hypnotized watching it pulse inward and outward and I was sure it was going to burst in a dramatic Baby Soft Spot Accident and that I would never be able to get the baby brains put back in the right order. He said soft spots aren't all that soft—and anyway, it would finally close up on its own and I should try to refrain from worrying over it for about eighteen more months.

Your two moms and the stuff they know that you don't

Believe me, they know plenty. The trouble is most of it was learned back in the Dark Ages before disposable diapers were gender-specific and before there were fourteen kinds of car seats. Some mothers were having children even before it was known, for instance, that babies aren't supposed to be as regimented as the United States Army when it comes to things like sleeping and eating, and that it was not okay to give them whiskey when they didn't sleep in the middle of the night.

Also, since the days when we were born, it has been discovered that dressing babies in layers and layers of blankets can make them hot, which is not necessarily a good thing. Some mothers back in the old days operated on the assumption that since babies lived inside other people for nine months, they expected temperatures always to be in the high nineties and would become distraught if it were, say, a cool 75 degrees. Scientists have now realized that babies don't like to be overheated any more than the rest of us and that they should not, for instance, wear snowsuits in the summer.

Good luck convincing your mom of this.

In fact, good luck convincing her of anything. Here's what she has over you: She raised you, and you lived. And now the ugly truth is that here you are, on your best days not at all sure that you can keep this infant alive, and she's already pulled off this marvelous feat.

Still, you have to somehow put your childhood behind you. Many women say they became best friends with their mothers once they had a baby themselves. It helps, I think, if you've already forgiven her for the fact that she made you wear your hair in braids for the school picture back in seventh grade, and in tenth grade she wouldn't let you paint your room black and purple. Unfortunately, if you haven't gotten to that marvelous point of forgiveness, there will most likely be a moment when you think you may have to strangle her just because she says something inflammatory like, "Dear, I really think the baby should wear a hat in the sun." You need to know that she's probably right.

But even if your mother is terrific, there most likely will still come a moment when it turns out she has some crazy notion of child care that is going to drive you completely insane. You'll discover that she believes, for instance, against all medical evidence, that babies who don't eat pablum by the age of six weeks have unsatisfactory social relationships when they're teenagers, or that she read somewhere that most serial killers used blue pacifiers. And you are going to have to correct her.

Mothers hate this more than anything. You can hardly make even the tiniest correction of them without getting a rise out of them. Even the simplest request, like, "Please be careful when you pick him up; we've been trying not to drop him on his head," can make your mother go crazy on you. She'll start telling you how, even back when she was a new mother, pediatricians were already recommending that babies not be dropped on their heads, and that she's lived whole decades of her life without ever dropping anyone on his head.

"Fine," you say. "I didn't think it would hurt to remind you."

Also, I was amazed at this, but it turned out there actually were some things that my mother knew that helped. After all, she had read Dr. Spock. And after I finally got finished making her understand that my social life in seventh grade was ruined by the fact that she hand-sewed a red-and-white gingham dress for me and made me wear it on picture day—well, once we got that out of the way, and she said she was truly sorry, then I found it easier to listen to things she had to say on the subject of new babies.

The crying

It is a well-known fact that babies cry, and yet for some reason, it is always a shock when it happens in your own home. You can't believe there is this incessant high-pitched noise—it's worse than the smoke alarm—that you can't get to stop. There is no little button on the underneath that will make this baby pipe down, and not even any batteries you can remove so you can get a good night's sleep. (Some people think the purpose of the pacifier is to plug up the hole that the crying is coming from, but babies hate this particular use of the pacifier. They see right through any attempt to shut them up, and they hold a grudge against the person who is doing it. I have seen the force of a single wail cause a pacifier to go hurling across the room, knocking over lamps and vases and smashing windows.)

You will spend a lot of time musing on the act of crying. You will try to analyze it, diagnose it, interpret its deep inner message, and mostly, try to make it stop. And you will be amazed to discover how many people have theories about crying that they are only too happy to share with you.

Why Is the Baby Crying becomes a game you can play right in your own living room, for endless hours. Technically, the participants in this game don't even have to be in the vicinity to join in. I've had friends and relatives call long-distance to contribute their ideas.

"Why is he crying? What have you done to him?" my mother asked once after a whole grueling five seconds of hearing the baby cry over the telephone line.

"I haven't done anything to him," I told her, sighing. "I'm trying to help him."

"Oh, yeah? And what have you done to help?"

"I nursed him, and—"

"You nursed him? Well, it's obvious what's going on. You don't have enough milk. Give him some cereal."

"He's too young for cereal. And the doctor said—"

"Nonsense. I gave you cereal when you were five days old, and you haven't stopped eating since. Slept right through the night at two weeks, potty trained at eleven months—the doctors said it couldn't be done. You start listening to doctors, and you'll find yourself with a screaming kid on your hands, day and night, straight through 'til he leaves for college."

"I'm not giving him cereal."

"Give him cereal."

"No cereal."

Silence. Then: "Put him on."

"He's two weeks old, Mom. He doesn't do phones yet."

"Put the phone up to his ear. Let me tell him a few things." Believe it or not, I was just desperate enough to do it. I don't know what she told him, but he looked startled to have this plastic thing put up against his red-faced, scrunched-up, screaming little head—and sure enough, about an hour later, he fell asleep, and she claimed full credit for it. It would have been sooner, she said, if I'd foresworn breast-feeding right then and there and switched to cereal.

Mothers aren't the only ones who know how to stop babies from crying. Perfect strangers, who have never seen you before, will gladly leap across supermarket displays and lose their place in line at banks to tell you all you need to know to solve the crying dilemma.

Many of them will very brightly suggest you change the baby's diaper, as if this is something that would never have occurred to you. These people will always call you honey or dear and will speak to you as though you are not quite all there mentally.

"How long has it been since you've changed his diaper, dear?" they will say, as though they expect that you

36

will smite your forehead and then fall to thanking them for their perceptiveness.

Now, I personally have never met a baby who cared one way or the other about the condition of the diaper, unless there was some huge rash situation down there, in which case the crying was pretty much all the time anyway and not just when the diaper was wet. Mostly, I think, babies would vote against diaper changes altogether, because it means having to lie down and have things done to them, and they can lose their train of thought and forget to cry as loudly.

But it is no use explaining this to helpful people in the supermarket. When you explain that all the baby maintenance work has been done—feeding, changing, clothing found to be just right and not too tight in any delicate areas—people will start dragging out their own family's crying remedies. These can be a lot of fun, if you're in the right mood, which you definitely are not and won't be for some time—until at least six months after the Crying Years are done. I had fun whipping out pieces of paper and writing down people's ideas. Sometimes it even made them go away.

Theories from Grocery Store Customers on How to Stop a Baby from Crying

- Hold it close to your heart and rock it sideways, singing "Toora Loora Loora" in the key of G, in a monotone that doesn't go over .5 decibels. Remember to roll your Rs when you say "Irish," or the whole deal is off.
- Stop eating garlic, onions, spices, and anything else that you really like. In fact, you must kick yourself for eating these things during your pregnancy, which was probably how the baby got this way in the first place.
- Put a heating pad on its feet. Do not turn it on high, however.

- Turn on the blow-dryer. This may actually work because the blow-dryer is so loud that it will probably drown out any crying sound, especially if you put it next to your ear. Even if the baby is still crying, at least your hair can get dry.
- Give it peppermint drops in its milk. (Tricky if you're breast-feeding.)
- Carry the baby like a football. Resist the urge to throw it.
- Threaten the kid with reform school if it hasn't stopped by the time it's ten.
- Change your own personality so that you are more relaxed, since obviously it is your own high-strung nature that has caused this to happen in the first place. Perhaps if you'd taken the trouble to get some psychotherapy for yourself before you thought of reproducing, then none of this would have come about.

Why you will never again be anywhere on time

Get used to the idea that nothing is ever again going to happen on time. Just give up on having any semblance of control over when events take place. You are simply never again going to get out of your house when you expect to. Sometimes—but only sometimes—the delay will be because the baby is crying or needs to nurse as you are running out the door. This is something you could explain to other people. But hardly ever is this what has gone wrong.

Mostly you will be late because of reasons you can't quite explain to anyone's satisfaction, most of all your own: One stroller wheel got inexplicably stuck in the backwards position and wouldn't budge and so you kicked it to dislodge it, only the whole stroller fell apart, with all four wheels rolling in different directions. Or the tapes on the diaper decided one day that they were not going to stick and so the diaper shunted out of the leg hole of the overalls when you picked the baby up. Or maybe it was that you looked in the mirror and realized that there were two gigantic wet circles on the front of your shirt, and so you had to dry them with the blow-dryer—and then, as you got to the car, you noticed that the baby had diarrhea in his hair.

By far the most disruptive things to the idea of a schedule are the Bodily Function Accidents (known as BFAs at our house), those times when poop, spit-up, or pee have gotten out of their rightful containment devices and somehow made it necessary for all of you to change clothes, and perhaps even reupholster the furniture and repaint the walls.

There is no scientific explanation for how this comes about, but there you will be, hand on the doorknob, ready to go out in the world and show yourself to be a decent, competent, well- dressed individual, who just happens to have a decent, competent, well-dressed infant person with you. And then there will be an unearthly sound, and within seconds, all hope of getting somewhere on time is ruined.

Naturally, most BFAs occur as you are leaving home or when you have managed to get yourself so far from home that going back there is an impossibility. You will find that hardly ever do they happen just as you are, say, arriving home from somewhere and are looking for a good reason to give yourself and the baby a bath. And the main thing about BFAs is not so much their deep aroma, an aroma so strong that you realize it threatens the well-being of anyone who might come within three blocks of you—but is the fact that they are accompanied by horrific stains, all in the brown spectrum.

My friend Lori once had a ten-week-old baby explode in a multiple BFA—that is, from both ends—at an airport as they were waiting to get on an airplane for a five-hour flight. Being a wise and practical parent, Lori had packed a change of clothes for the baby in the trusty diaper bag, but unfortunately she had nothing for herself to change into. She

39

said later that the only advantage was that she and the baby got practically an entire section of the plane to themselves. Still, it stopped just short of being worth it, and Lori later learned how to fold her own clothing so small that she could just about carry it in her wallet. Needless to say, she has never so much as gone to the grocery store without taking most of her wardrobe with her.

But back to schedules: There are some other reasons they don't work. One is that, in your newly addled state of being a new parent, you probably won't be able to remember what happens from one day to the next. Nature releases a whole bunch of fog-inducing hormones when you get a new baby because, if you were in your right mind, you would never be able to tolerate what is happening in your day-to-day life.

This is what would always happen to me: I'd have a medium-okay day with the baby, meaning that in one twenty-four-hour period, we both eventually became dressed, fed, and had a bearable amount of sleep—and I'd think, "Aha! So this is what life is supposed to be like! A schedule! We're going to do it exactly this way every day from now on."

But then the next day I couldn't remember whether we'd eaten our fourth snack before we'd gotten dressed or afterwards—and besides that, unlike the day before when there were a mere sixteen interruptions, the phone on the second day would ring twenty-seven times in one morning from people wanting to offer me new telephone plans or aluminum siding, and by the time I got back to my life, I had lost total track of where I was in the schedule.

I'm aware that others don't have these problems. My friend Julie was a marvel of scheduling. Ask her what time her three-month-old daughter had a juice break, and Julie rattled off that juice was always presented at 10:20 A.M. and then again at 4:20 P.M. And by God, if you were there at those times, you'd see her whip out a bottle of apple juice and plug it into the kid's mouth, whether the kid was thirsty or not.

"What if something else is going on at those times?" I asked her once. "What if, say, you happened to be on the toilet?"

She looked shocked. "Well, of course, I wouldn't be," she said.

I don't know how one gets such a life. Let's say you do manage to do something one day, and then, amazing yourself and others, you also manage to pretty much duplicate that on the following day. Stretch your mind, and imagine that you even can go for a whole two weeks with basically the same bedtime, feeding, and juice events happening within, say, a half-hour range of each other. You may not want to call this a schedule just yet, but still, things are shaping up nicely. You sort of know when the baby will take a nap and when she will wake up and at which points of the day and night you are going to want to have your breasts unoccupied and available.

That's when the authorities decide to change either from or to Daylight Savings Time.

No one is really sure whether it's easier to have a baby in Daylight Time or that other kind of time. And it's even more impossible to figure out what the change is likely to do to your schedule. Once my friend Kate and I wasted a perfectly good visit trying to decide if our babies were likely to wake up earlier or later than usual, now that the time change was upon us. We couldn't do it.

Kate thought that because there would be an extra hour in the day, the baby would probably sleep later because it would be darker in his room, but I thought an extra hour represented just a golden opportunity to get in some more crying time even earlier than usual, and that there wasn't a baby in America who could withstand that temptation. We finally agreed to call each other the next day with a report on what had happened.

Both babies, however, had been drooling all over the same toys while we debated the issue, and the next morning they both had fevers and colds and spent most of the morning screaming. So I still don't know. To me, it is just another reason that people with small children can never get a schedule to work for them.

The parents you meet in the park

It's time to talk about the other people you will encounter now that you have a baby. People you never would have paid any attention to before, mainly because they had chocolate smeared all over the front of their business suits, are now candidates to become your best friends. You will actually seek out people who have the same frazzled look in their eyes that you see in your own mirror, and you will find yourself thinking that, damn it, chocolate does have a place on the front of a business suit. It denotes a kind of casualness about attire that the whole world should be looking to emulate.

No, you will never again be so happy to see other adults in your life as when you have a baby at home. They represent sanity, civilization, conversation, and in most cases, they are the only people you will see all day who are not looking to pee or spit up on you. Also, they don't intentionally drop objects just to watch you pick them up, and they hardly ever rip at your clothing to get at your breasts so you will give them a snack.

Still, there's something about them that I have to tell you. They do not think your baby is the most amazing baby in the playground.

You will be at the park, telling them some fascinating story about how your baby very athletically and with total physical coordination and muscle control managed to reach for his toes and then, with all the precision of an Olympic gymnast, brought his entire foot to his mouth, and inserted his big toe there. And—I don't know how to soften this for you—they will not care.

Somebody will say, practically stifling a yawn, "My Joey could put an entire bureau in his mouth when he was your kid's age."

And somebody else will say, "So, how old's your kid anyway? Five months? My twins, who, by the way, were called Premature Medical Miracles by the doctors, were able to walk at five months, as long as you held onto their hands. And one of them actually asked to use the potty when he was five months and two weeks. I swear to God."

Other babies at the park, you will learn, could recognize all the Sesame Street characters from the age of three weeks, had managed to climb out of their bassinets before the hospital had signed them out from birth, and now that they are eleven months old can recite the Iranian alphabet and may be asked to consult on filling out their parents' tax forms. Yeah, and Yale and Harvard are already mailing out informational brochures for their proposed toddler undergraduate programs.

And as for physical adorability, so what that your baby has pillowy pink cheeks and lashes that could knock over block towers? There's not going to be a single baby in the park who hasn't been approached by a modeling agency and could be making millions right this very minute, except that their mothers think they deserve normal childhoods and some fresh air every once in a while.

There will be days you will push the stroller home from the park and think life would probably work for you if only you had thought to pack a bottle of gin in the diaper bag before you left home. You will wonder how it was that simply having a baby got you mixed up with such weird people, and what you could possibly do to extricate yourself from all these relationships.

But then you'll go home and cuddle the baby and cook supper. And later the baby will smile from her high

43

chair, where she's just discovered that she can transport Cheerios to her mouth by sticking them to her drool-soaked palms, and you'll see for yourself that she's an actual genius, not that it matters, because you are completely and utterly under her spell, and even if this is the last thing she ever manages to accomplish in childhood and she has to live with you the rest of her life because no one else ever sees how brilliant and perceptive she is, it's enough, it really is enough because she is yours.

Which, of course, isn't the way it's going to turn out anyway.

Things Not to Discuss With the Parents in the Park

- The incredible physical feats of strength your baby can already perform.
- What they possibly could have been thinking when they named their baby Theophilus Emmanuel.
- The fact that you think their child is probably a potentially dangerous criminal because of the way he likes to dump sand in all the other kids' eyes.
- How much weight you gained during pregnancy. (Everyone always subtracts at least ten pounds.)
- Your theory that toilet training can wait until the advanced age of three.
- Your babysitter's phone number.

The mommy club

Still, there is no way around it. You're now part of the Motherhood Sisterhood, and the time will come when you realize that the women you meet on the playground or at the Mommy and Me exercise class are destined to be your very best friends. So what if they don't admire your baby as much as you do? They, after all, are the only ones to whom you can confess that your baby eats junk mail, and that you ate two pounds of buttered noodles and cried three times the day before. Chances are, the same things were going on in their houses.

Other mothers are also the only people who can understand what's going on between you and your husband: how it is that you have to renegotiate the housework deal with him, now that it includes baby care. At my play group, we all agreed that getting men to change diapers was our ultimate goal. And then we got hysterical talking about the lengths a man will go to simply to pretend he doesn't smell an obviously poopy diaper. One man had turned up the baseball game extra loud and claimed that his nose didn't work so well when his ears were being overtaxed that way.

As with all deep friendships, these will come to have their little code words of understanding. After the first week, you will never again have to be specific about anything. You can just say, "Husband," and your new sisterhood friends will groan and nod in understanding. Other words that will work just as well are babysitter, boss, colic, teething, diarrhea.

Nothing brings people together like the shared experience of trying to figure out parenthood. It was my friend Liza who explained to me that a foolproof way of getting a cranky baby to sleep was to drive around the block thirteen times, while singing "Love Me Tender" in a voice that got progressively softer. Then, she said, you should sit in the car, read a good book, and drink some iced tea until the nap was over. If the baby stirred or appeared to be waking up, Liza said to start bouncing in the seat to make the car move again, and—if you can—make some motor noises. She said you should never try to do fewer than thirteen trips, and never ever attempt to take the baby out of the car seat once he had fallen asleep.

You see, that's the kind of information you're just not going to find anywhere else.

Your old friends—you know, the ones who haven't had kids yet

Okay, so they're always saying, "We've got to get together." Here's the thing they don't know: You need to be home by 7:30.

P.M., that is.

You need to. That's all there is to it.

Of course it's not because you have a new baby and you want to sit and admire him at every moment. You are totally capable of being away from the baby for many periods of time—eons, practically—at least, lots more than your childless friends give you credit for. And it's not because you haven't been able to find a suitably certified babysitter either, including several registered nurses and your mother. It's not even the breast-feeding thing.

It's because 7:45 is pretty much your new bedtime. And what of it?

This, you see, is just another one of the marvelous things having a new baby does for you: You realize for the first time in your life that sleep is all that is keeping most of the people on the planet tethered to reality. You see with a hard clarity that really—besides maybe air—nothing else matters as much as closing your eyes. Food is secondary, sex is way down the list, talking to friends, even stuff you used to think was pretty important like bathing and brushing your teeth—they're nothing compared to the pleasure of sleep.

Like veterans reminiscing about World War II, new mothers can get teary-eyed remembering the blessed nights when five hours slipped by while they were still unconscious. I got so carried away with my desire for sleep that I once thought it was a shame they didn't make commercials for it on television. I mean, who knew how precious a commodity it was?

Try telling this to a childless person, however.

My friend Sarah, a person who had not gotten around to having kids of her own yet and so didn't know that there is

46

such a thing as sleep deprivation, once said to me, "You go to bed at 7:45 and yet you always have dark circles under your eyes. Maybe you're getting too much sleep."

This, of course, is a very childless person thing to say, and is just one of the reasons it's no longer fun to go to childless people's parties. They catch you slumping over the tray of hors d'oeuvres or curled up in their bathtub, and you won't hear the end of it anytime soon. Yet, it's still considered a criminal offense to punch them out. You just have to try to manage a bleary, watery smile in their direction and pray that their birth control devices fail them while you're still young enough to appreciate it.

Then there is the way they roll their eyes when you tell them something about the baby. You can't tell them anything. If you complain about how the baby keeps you up all night but then boast a little about how you've learned to sleep with one arm draped over the bassinet and clamped down on the pacifier, a childless person will say something like, "Seems to me a baby needs to learn to put his pacifier in all by himself."

And then you'll say, in a friendly and educational sort of tone, "Well, at five weeks of age, there's hardly anything they can do for themselves. They can't even find their own hands yet."

And the C.P. will say, "Is that right? Well, maybe special schools will be necessary somewhere down the line. Say, did you know that China is the number-two producer of camel hair paintbrushes in the world?"

Actually, it pays to be grateful for the way they change the subject when you say anything about the baby. What's worse is when they tell you their theories about children. C.P.s have a lot of theories, none of them having ever been tested on real human subjects, of course.

But get them started, and they will tell you why their unborn child won't be crying in the middle of the night or addicted to some stupid plastic device like a pacifier.

Once, hearing the pacifier referred to in such a disparaging way, I got tears in my eyes. "The pacifier," I cried, "is in contention for the world's most valuable invention and the greatest contributor to international peace! Whoever invented the pacifier should have gotten the Nobel prize! If it weren't for the binky, I wouldn't be even the half person I am today!"

This, of course, was a major error. (Okay, okay—so I can't put it on my resume that I never used that word.) I was a little tired when I said it. One should never speak the Sacred Baby Jargon in front of the non-initiates. I saw, too late, my friend's eyes go wild and her face blanch.

"The—what did you say?"

"Nothing. Nothing. It was a slip of the tongue."

"You said binky."

"I would never say that word. No, no, I didn't say it. I didn't."

"You're turning into—one of those people, aren't you? The kind of people who have a whole new weird language all to themselves."

I shrugged. Then I said, "Well, as long as the barrier's been broken, let me tell you about the umbilical stump and the onesies. And did you know that the baby just last night managed to suck on his toe for about two and a half minutes?"

Here's something, though, that it pays to keep in mind if you're going to have to consort with C.P.s. Their fertility and stamina are still untested, and at some level—admittedly, it may be very deep down, but still it's there—they are jealous of you. And they are also afraid of losing you, afraid that you're going to start confiding in your new baby and not love them anymore, and that secretly, while you're up in the middle of the night, you are thinking what a better person you are than they are, all because you've reproduced.

That's how silly they are. When you are up in the middle of the night, the only thing you are thinking is how to get back into your bed. Everyone should know that. But C.P.s forget. They think you're being smug when you toss out little terms like binky and projectile vomiting. They don't want to give you any points for heroism just because you were in labor fifty million hours while you existed on sour lollipops and a couple of ice chips. (Above all, they're jealous that you found a way to lose twenty pounds in a couple of hours.)

If you want to make a C.P feel good, tell her that you think labor is a hell of a tough way to lose twenty pounds, and that you'll never tell your baby one secret you haven't told her first.

And then tell her that if she ever says, "When I have a kid, he certainly isn't ever going to behave like yours!" you'll sneak into her bathroom and poke holes in her diaphragm.

The great fun of baby talk

One of the best parts about having a baby is that you get to talk to them. You're even supposed to. Doctors and researchers, and even your mother, all agree that it's quite important that you talk to your baby as much as possible, so they get the idea that talking is an okay thing to do, and it inspires them to someday achieve this for themselves— perhaps so they can argue with you.

But don't think about those future arguments now. For quite a long time, you get to do all the talking, and they listen to you with an expression on their faces that says, "This is the most amazing person in the whole world, to be able to make these incredible noises with that opening in her face. How does she do it?"

This is one of the best feelings there is—and one that you may want to call up your childless friends to report on. That way, other times when you call them up wailing because your life is so out of control now that you have an infant, they can remind you that you once said it was fun to talk to babies. That's what friends are for, after all.

Many people will try to tell you there is a right way and a wrong way to talk to babies. There isn't. You get to say anything you want, in any drippy tone of voice you want. So what if you happen to like saying, "Is dis da fweet widda baby who fwowed up all over mama's fweater?" I say, whose business is it—as long as you have made sure to turn the baby monitor off, so your downstairs guests aren't hearing this and laughing at you behind your back.

It's damn near impossible to talk to babies in a regular tone of voice anyway. And I think talking in a high, falsetto voice is useful because it keeps you from telling the baby distressing things, like about the Middle East political situation, and the national debt, and the theories behind supply-side economics. You don't want babies to guess that life on this planet is any worse than the occasional wet diaper or gas bubble.

The best thing about talking to babies is that they are a great audience. All three of mine thought that I was a comedic genius because I knew how to say the words "boozha boozha boozha" while shaking my hair a few inches above their heads. Apparently boozha is the most hilarious word ever invented in baby language, because I later discovered I could get a laugh just by saying it, conversationally, to a baby who was riding, bored, in a car seat. I really think there should be baby comedians who go on TV and wag their heads while they say things like, "How about those boozha boozhas, kids?"

The thing about baby talk, though, is knowing when to stop. One day it's no longer amusing to hear about "fwow up" or "the fweet widda baby." Don't worry; you'll know when that day comes, just by instinct. And it won't be as the kid is packing his duffel bag for college, either. You'll just realize, sooner rather than later, that you don't want your toddler walking around saying the wrong names for things, and so you'll start speaking in very precise, almost scientific ways.

"Mommy's sweater—suh-wett-err—is blue. Ba. Lue. And your name is Ryan. Ry. An. And you are seventeen months old. Say sev-en-teen."

There used to be a woman in our neighborhood who ran an in-home day-care center for toddlers, and we all used to love to hear her talk to them outside. She would discuss things with them as though it were a convening of the United Nations, rather than a play group.

"Now, what are we going to do about Joey's perception that there's a scarcity of tricycles?" she'd say in the most matter-of-fact voice imaginable. "I say that maybe this weekend my husband is going to have to go out and purchase some other vehicles for this establishment, but in the meantime, let's agree to a few ground rules, shall we? How about no more than twenty minutes per child on a tricycle, and then we rotate to allow others? The ones not on a vehicle can play in the sandbox."

Sure enough, two trikeless kids would trudge off to the sandbox to wait their turn—while those of us eavesdropping from afar would drop our jaws in wonder.

All I can say is those kids today are probably running the U.N., while at my house, we all still think "boozha boozha" is about the funniest thing going.

Chapter 3: Why Babies Cry

A lot of research has gone into the question of what makes babies suddenly get hysterical and start shrieking as though the end of the world is coming. It's not always hunger pangs or the discomfort of a wet diaper, you know. It's not even necessarily the dreaded ear infection or stomachache.

Babies have a lot of good reasons to cry. After extensive research, scientists working with very sensitive cause-detecting instruments have listed the following possible reasons your baby won't shut up:

- The air currents in the room are brushing up against his cheek in a way that reminds him of the impermanence and instability of earthly existence.
- The tape on his diaper is sticking to his skin instead.
- He is tired of the work of growing eyelashes.
- He wishes he could talk already.
- He's bored by life.
- He feels that riding backwards in his car seat is a violation of his civil rights.
- He doesn't like the pattern on the crib bumper pads.
- He can't remember where his thumb is or how to get it to his lips.
- He senses that each and every time he has to have a shirt put on him, it's going to be like getting born all over again.

- He thinks that a hundred times around the dining room table on your shoulder is a pitifully small number, and he wishes he'd been born to someone who really could commit to walking a baby.
- His earlobes are bent under while he's lying down.
- He's fairly certain that his arms and legs are going to fly off, now that he's not still living in a tight little space.
- He thinks that when you suction his nose, you're really after his brains.
- He smelled chocolate on your breath, and he's fairly certain you're holding out on him, food-wise.
- He thought the deal was that he got to sleep right next to you all the time, not just when you felt like it.
- He's heard the rumors about cats wanting to suck the breath of tiny babies. The cat told him.
- He senses a distinction between pacifiers and the one you have just given him is his least favorite.
- The stuffed animals you've decorated his crib with are terrifying him, and he wants them hurled overboard.
- It's tough being an entity in a body that you don't yet have the instruction manual for.
- He's gathered that you two are novices, and he'd like some experienced parents shipped in.
- He wonders if one of these days, you're going to expect him to breast-feed you, and he's pretty sure he doesn't have enough milk.
- He's still mad about that umbilical thing falling off, and he wonders if the fingers and toes will be the next to go.
- He has no confidence in the pediatrician you chose.
- He was insulted when he overheard someone say he has a nose like his grandfather.

- All in all, he liked the womb better. This having to remember to breathe is really a drag.
- He's vaguely aware that someday someone is going to ask him how electricity gets into the walls and what the advantages are of a bicameral government, and he doesn't know how to find out.
- He heard another baby sneeze in the hospital nursery, and he's not sure he knows how to do that.
- He can't remember his own name.
- He knows that he looks like Dwight Eisenhower.
- He thought everybody got issued ten toes on each foot, and now he feels he got shortchanged.
- He's wondering why there aren't more little people around, like in the hospital.
- He's not sure who you're supposed to complain to when things aren't working out.
- He bit his tongue.

Chapter 4:
Don't Let the Paraphernalia Get You Down

What a seven-pounder needs to get by

You're not going to believe the amount of stuff you're now going to own as a parent of an infant. It's not stuff you ever really thought you wanted, either—not the boats and Porsches and white leather couches you might have pictured for yourself. It's all the paraphernalia needed to raise a child these days: the cribs, swings, exercisers, mobiles, toys, gadgets, gimmicks, and containment devices that make up daily life for a baby.

These items just creep into your life. One day it seems you are still able to walk freely through your house, and the next—even though your child still weighs only about seven pounds and takes up approximately twenty-one inches of your household space— you realize that you can't walk through any room without stubbing your toe on a few baby supplies, and that you also can't open any drawer without pacifiers, diaper covers, thermometers, nail clippers, and at least one nasal suction apparatus spilling out on you.

Somehow, when you weren't looking, you have moved into a juvenile furniture showroom.

What's worse is that a great deal of this stuff has to go with you whenever you go anywhere. I remember the night some friends invited us over for dinner when our first child was about five months old. It was the first time we came face-to-face with the fact that, as a family of three, we couldn't go anywhere without taking two cars.

We needed the diaper bag, of course, and the portacrib—because you never know if the kid will need to fall asleep—and the stroller, in case we decided to take a walk, the high chair (the clip-on, travel high chair, not the one we had in our kitchen), a pad for changing diapers on the floor, changes of clothes for all of us (because one BFA can take out the lot of you), the windup swing (because it was the only way to get him to go to sleep), rattles, teething rings, a Busy Box, an exerciser to hang in the doorway (in case he got restless during dinner), the nasal suction apparatus (the kid had a cold), a baby seat (for him to sit in on the table while we ate, in case he wasn't restless after all), wipes, a washcloth, plastic bags to put soiled things in, a thermometer (in case his temperature spiked), a bottle of juice, and four or five pacifiers (because they tend to get lost).

After we got everything unpacked and set up in their living room, I said, "Whew! I don't know how people who aren't nursing go anywhere. Just think how much more stuff we'd have to bring along if I weren't breast-feeding."

They said, "You didn't bring this much stuff with you three years ago when we went camping for two weeks."

It's true. It's almost a law that the smaller the member of the household, the more junk she has to have hauled for her on trips. You just have to face it that your days of traveling light are gone. In fact, your days of traveling without a Mack truck may be gone.

Baby catalogs

It's obvious that the blame lies with baby catalogs. As soon as you even begin thinking about having a baby, these start coming in the mail. My theory is that baby paraphernalia companies have monitors in our birth control devices—and just as soon as a condom with a hole in it gets sold, alarms go off in their company headquarters, and the next thing you know, you're pregnant and a catalog for baby objects arrives at your house. I think, in fact, the paraphernalia companies may actually be the first to know your good news.

Needless to say, when our mothers were having us, they didn't have nearly the choices of stuff to purchase. All they got to buy was a crib, a stroller, a pile of cotton diapers, and possibly a pacifier. If they were really extravagant, they might have gone for the crib bumpers to keep us from banging our little heads on the bars. But that was pretty much it. Many mothers from that era will still try to convince you this is all you need. They will even tell you that if you don't feel like buying a crib, you can use a cardboard box for a long time without any bad effects.

Please. Give me a break. No one who has ever peeked inside a catalog and seen that there is a teddy bear who sings your baby to sleep with a Brahms lullaby and then gradually dims the lights is going to settle for the Cardboard Box Style of Parenting. I mean, *I* don't even know how to gradually dim the lights, so I'm very impressed by a stuffed animal that can manage it. Or how about the special video camera that scans the baby's room so you don't have to keep getting up and going in to check on her? That way, you can watch television and then click over to the Baby's Room Channel and see what's happening in there. (After watching the news for a few minutes, you may decide that you only want to watch the Baby's Room Channel. After all, it has all the suspense of a drama: Will the baby stay asleep even though he's snuffling? Will he continue breathing through the night? And, really—should you have gone with the wallpaper with the yellow ducks?) Without a baby catalog, you might never know you needed to think about these questions.

Clearly, baby catalogs are of the opinion that we need something for every imaginable worry of child raising. Surely you've been sitting up nights trying to think of a way to wipe your baby's bottom without using those hysterically cold packaged wipes. Forget going for a warm washcloth. Why should you, when there's a simple little device you can plug in and have the whole box of wipes prewarmed?

Or, if you're nursing and are worrying about how you'll keep any excess pumped milk from spoiling, you can buy a Lac-Tote, a three-pound refrigerator to carry in your purse (assuming your purse is a suitcase) for those annoying times when you have a lot of milk but the baby's not around to drink it up.

Don't know any good lullabies? There really are teddy bears that play Brahms lullabies for fifteen minutes while the light gradually dims—and that will start to automatically play again if the baby cries in the middle of the night. And cribs that know how to start rocking when your little one wakes up in the night and just would like a little motion to make things fine again.

Let's say you are the curious type who would like to know what your baby's temperature is most of the time; there's now a pacifier that will display it for you. And there are little visor-type hats that will keep shampoo out of her eyes when you're washing her hair, cuff holders to keep her from tripping on her baggy blanket sleepers once she starts walking, and—for you—a system so you can carry along a drink for yourself while you're using two hands to push the stroller. There may be days when you need a gin and tonic to take along on a walk with the baby, and it's good that catalog companies can anticipate that you can't very well push the stroller, have your nervous breakdown, and carry an alcoholic beverage all at the same time.

Parenthood has other dangers as well. Perhaps it's the bathtub that makes you feel you've gotten yourself into a dangerous, tricky situation and should not have been allowed to reproduce after all. Besides the shampoo-in-the-eyes problems, there's the fact that the tub is a rock-hard, freezing-cold block of porcelain, just waiting for a baby's delicate anatomy to crash on it. Don't worry. You can purchase a special waterproof vinyl pad that will not only cushion it, but will keep it warm so that your child can perhaps make it to adolescence without ever having to experience how really cold the side of the bathtub can be.

Obviously you can't fill up your house with all this stuff. Even if you had the money, you probably don't have that much storage room. Besides, I think it's best that infants learn slowly that life is filled with hard edges and cold wipes. If you don't let them learn for themselves, the only intimation they'll get that life is not a bed of true comfort is when you trip over all this paraphernalia and yell, "Oh, shit!"

He's gotta have it

Still, there are things you are probably going to have to buy. Because it can be scary going into a baby furniture store, I feel I should make a list of the things you really must get, apart from all the weird things the catalog companies want to entice you with.

The Crib: The first thing to know is that no baby has ever appreciated a crib. This is because it's obvious to babies that cribs are really legalized cages designed to keep them in one place. Babies as young as three weeks old know that the rest of the population doesn't typically sleep behind bars, and they resent the implication that you don't trust them. I'm sorry, but a baby placed in such a prison—and what choice do you really have, after all?—feels very strongly that it will be necessary to stay awake and on guard at all times, even through the most compelling drowsiness.

Bassinet: Okay, for a very short while, you can use a bassinet instead. This is a flimsy device, like an oval-shaped cardboard box on legs, that for some reason babies think is acceptable. My theory is that they approve of bassinets because they surmise that bassinets aren't as sturdy as cribs and so they have every hope of someday being able to beat their way out of them and escape. You will come in sometimes and see your little five-week-old baby looking around at the walls of the bassinet. He is taking measurements, planning for the day when he will catapult to freedom. Little does he realize that long before that day comes, you will have consigned him to a place behind bars, where he can be safely contained.

Crib Bumpers: Most parents, feeling slightly bad about the baby-behind-bars concept, try to disguise the jail-like appearance of the crib by padding the edges with bright-colored, tie-on bumpers. This is a good idea even though it doesn't fool babies for even one tiny second. At least it keeps them from knocking their little heads against the bars in their many attempts to slide through. (They can't actually slide through the bars, but this doesn't keep them from trying.) After a certain age, babies will rip the bumper pads away from the bars and use them as weapons to hurl at you; still later, many babies will stand on them, in the hopes that they can finally reach the top of the crib and leap over the side.

The Stroller: Once you realize that you can't carry the baby around forever in your arms, you see that you will need a device with wheels on it. The trouble is, there are about a million designs of such things. Some strollers these days claim that they can also be car seats, beds, and high chairs, when they're not otherwise busy with you on the sidewalk. I don't think you want to get into this; it's like the Swiss army knife approach to baby furniture. Pretty soon, if life continues this way, companies will claim that all you have to buy is one piece of furniture, and it will somehow transform itself from crib to high chair to potty seat to car seat to stroller at the touch of a button. But you and I both know that that button will someday get stuck, and the day will come when you're strolling the kid around the streets in a potty chair, and people are pointing at you.

Choosing a stroller is a lot like picking a spouse. You will find it takes just as many hours of deep consideration and self-examination, the major difference being that your friends aren't going to be as interested in listening to you yammer on about the pros and cons of each individual model, the way they were when the subject was men.

What you need to know is this: There are strollers that are no bigger than umbrellas and that you can—theoretically, at least—include in that suitcase you're calling your purse lately. Then there are strollers that are so gigantic they could transport the military, and that probably have rack-and-pinion steering, shock absorbers, and air brakes. The Cadillacs of these types of strollers also have seating options that include the baby facing either forward or backwards, depending on whether he'd like to see you or do some sight-seeing—and all kinds of positions, everything from lying down to sitting fully upright. Be aware that the lying-down position is hated by babies everywhere. If babies were designing strollers, I think they would have compartments where they are suspended upright, as though on the bow of a ship, and could direct the course of the ride merely by their whims.

Snugli: This is yet another Infant Containment Device, one that fastens onto the front of you and lets you carry the baby right next to your chest. Only a very young baby will put up with the Snugli treatment because, with its close quarters, it makes them think that life in the new world has gotten canceled after all, and they won a trip back to the womb. This makes them very happy—and very sleepy.

Backpack: Really, these should come with medical warnings on them. I've never met anyone who could wear one for longer than twenty seconds without calling for anesthesia, which is hard to come by without checking yourself into a hospital. Even though they have padded straps, padded seats, and aluminum frames that claim to distribute the weight evenly, what it comes down to is that we're not designed to carry small people on our backs for more than one minute, tops.

Naturally, however, babies are very excited by backpacks because they believe themselves to be in the driver's seat when they are riding around in one. Because they can see over your shoulder, they see you in the role of pack animal and themselves as sultans. If you don't go where they wish you would, they know that they can pummel your kidneys and hip bones with their tough little heels, pull your hair, and chew on your ears until they get you to take the thing off.

Car Seat: Many years ago, believe it or not, cars weren't seen as the hideously dangerous, high-speed objects that they are today, and babies rode in them unencumbered by restraining devices. Mostly they lay on the seat next to the driver and rolled off at every stop sign, unless the driver flung an arm out and prevented this. My mother still today throws out her right arm whenever she's driving and I'm the passenger in her car.

These days it's considered a misdemeanor to let babies fall on the floor while you're driving—hospitals won't even let you take your new baby home until you produce a car seat for their inspection—and so a whole new industry has been born. All you really need to know is this: Little babies sit in the equivalent of a padded bucket and have to face backwards in the car (which they hate). After they get to be about twenty pounds, their reward is that they get to face forward and look out the window, although they still hate it because every inch of their bodies is strapped and pinned down to the seat.

Oh, yes, and one other bad part: You're supposed to bolt the thing to the frame of your car somehow, which causes a lot of swearing on the part of the person looking for a suitable bolting location. And when all that's done, you need to learn how to insert the baby into the seat while leaning into the car at an impossible angle and connect all the straps and buckles, keeping in mind that your major goal is that neither you nor the baby will come away with any permanent injuries. This gets to be almost a miraculous feat when the baby reaches about twelve pounds.

Windup Swing: This was invented so that parents don't starve to death during those early months, so you can't afford to go without one for very long—even if you're thinking of dieting. Here's how they work: You put the baby in the little seat and wind up the crank, and the swing then rocks her for a little while. You, meanwhile, must cook, eat, clean house, and anything else you can't do with a baby in your arms. It's a fabulous system.

The only thing you need to know is that the swing will wind down rather suddenly, and if your baby is like most others, she will wake up in a grouchy mood over the abruptness of her situation. Don't think you can just walk over and rewind the thing either. That will madden her beyond belief—because the noise of the crank is approximately the same decibel level as a helicopter landing on the roof of your house, not something a rudely awakened person is going to smile about. To solve this problem, you will have to learn a very delicate maneuver: You will have to rewind the baby swing before it comes to a complete halt. And you will have to do it by turning it one-quarter turn for each forward swing that it takes, so that the noise coincides with the click-click-click the swing makes. This sounds complicated, but you'll get so good at it that you could give seminars on baby swing winding in furniture stores and at showers, should your employment outlook change.

Pacifier: A household cannot own too many pacifiers. Having spent years chasing pacifiers as they scampered underneath furniture, tried to leap out of moving vehicles, and hunkered down to spend the winters behind the refrigerator, I can tell you there's no desperation quite like that you feel in the middle of the night when the current pacifier is vacationing elsewhere.

I think you need a minimum of fifteen pacifiers—and this is if you are a fairly organized, nonspacey kind of person to begin with. If, however, you have lost your house keys more than three times a year, even before you had a baby, then you are probably going to need to invest heavily in pacifiers—or orthodontic exercisers, as some of the uppity brands like to be referred to. At the barest minimum, I think you need two for each of the family cars (the glove compartment and the dashboard both need at least one), one each for your bedroom, the baby's room, the living room, the kitchen, the stroller, two to be carried in your pockets at all times, and two for your husband's pockets. I realize this is a hell of a lot of pacifiers, but even with that many, there will be no given day in which you can lay your hands on more than one of them.

The Layette: Frankly, no one under the age of sixty knows what this word refers to, and we're all too insecure to ask what it really means so we can decide if we really need to get one. Apparently it used to be a very hot item when our mothers' generation was getting born, because you will always hear older people inquiring as to the condition of your layette, as in, did you get one yet? And is it a nice one, and will you be passing it down to other babies, or putting it in storage when you're done with it? (The correct answers are: yes, yes, and storage. Layettes are sentimental items that you'll want to see again in the attic in twenty years.)

As near as I can tell, the layette (which has a vaguely illicit sound to it) really is just a fancy word for baby clothes and blankets, but to call it a layette makes it sound like something you could just go into a store and buy. Like my friend Jeanne, you might even look in the yellow pages, expecting to find Layettes R Us or Layette Depot stores. You won't.

From my informal research (which I accomplished without asking any questions whatsoever), layettes seem to be composed of all those things—onesies, receiving blankets, towels with little hoods built into them, and washcloths—that other people are supposed to give you. I think it's technically a baby shower item, purchasable as a unit only in stores that cater to attendees of baby showers. The rule is: People buy you layettes. You, I'm afraid, must buy baby clothes.

Various Baby Oils, Creams, Powders, and Ointments: You will not have a baby for longer than ten minutes before people are thinking up ways to make your baby shinier and more fragrant than it would otherwise be. Call me crazy, but I happen to like that slightly rancid baby smell. However, it's good to invest in a couple of ointments for when diaper rash strikes—and something perfumey for when company's on the way.

The baby monitor: the most dangerous device of all

Although most of your baby equipment will be on your side and will try to make life easier for you, I feel I must warn you that one item is determined to do you in. This is the baby monitor.

Oh, it seems to be helpful enough in its way. The whole idea is that you can be in another room and the monitor will let you eavesdrop on all the shenanigans that might be going on in your kid's room—things like the snoring, sucking, rumbling, crying, and screaming that you might like to know about, even though you're not right there. Having a baby monitor gives you more of a life: You get to floss your teeth, play with the dog, or even sleep without having to hang out full-time outside the baby's door. In the old days, before we had electronic devices, you'd see parents running back and forth to see if the baby had waked up yet— or else, pathetically, camped outside the door, trying to catch a nap for themselves by leaning on the doorjamb.

But baby monitors are hostile pieces of machinery, after all, like many of the other inanimate objects we allow into our lives. Just when you get where you trust them, they will play the most wicked tricks you can imagine. For one thing, they lull you into leaving them on all the time—and then, when you've totally forgotten that you're allowing your household to have electronic surveillance, one of your neighbors may casually happen to mention that it's too bad that you and your husband are arguing so much lately, and that he might want to try an antacid to help with his unfortunate, loud digestive problem late at night.

That's when you know that your baby monitor has been playing to an audience, broadcasting your personal life to anyone who got on your frequency. No one knows for sure how this happens. Hell, for all I know, it could be that your family's belches and disagreements are being transmitted over radio stations, for the population at large to hear.

As if this isn't disturbing enough, sometimes the monitor will decide to start broadcasting other people's lives for your listening enjoyment—usually around three or four in the morning, which is a time that I find electronic devices seem to get interested in stirring up some excitement. I once bolted wide awake, hearing a guy's voice suddenly, out of the darkness, arguing for me to sleep with him. He loudly listed his reasons, which included the information that he had a heart-shaped water bed and had recently invested in some plaid condoms that he was sure I would find very cool.

I glanced over at my snoring husband, wondering if he was going to put up with a burglar talking to me this way—and then realized that it was a voice from the baby monitor, obviously a man somewhere on a cellular phone talking to his girlfriend. The baby monitor didn't see fit to let us hear what her answer was—although later I had to guess that the plaid condoms had not been a particularly thrilling incentive.

I'm sure I don't have to point out to you that this is not the kind of entertainment that you can just get from any television show. You almost have to invest in a baby monitor in order to hear real-life seduction scenes in your life. The trouble is, often you would prefer not to hear the depressing things that pass for romance these days—and anyway, if it's possible, you'd probably much rather sleep.

The baby book

It may shock you to realize that, in addition to writing thank-you notes for your various layettes, you are also expected to be documenting your baby-producing experiences for posterity. This is just another example of the kind of thing no one tells you when you're still trying to decide if you're a person who can handle parenthood. For some of us, that would be the deal breaker right there: "Oh, yes, and in addition to living on twenty minutes of sleep a week, spending all your free time tracking down errant pacifiers, and remembering not to talk dirty in front of the baby monitor, you have to keep a baby book."

The baby book, in case you're wondering, is supposedly a scrapbook of everything you and the baby have gone through together since birth—all the good parts, at least. I have found, in my own life at least, that it's nice if you can manage to resist writing The True Story of Projectile Vomiting, and The Day the Screaming Lasted Far into the Night. Your child will later thank you.

And while not exactly being a journal of lies, let's just say that the baby book traditionally is not the place for all the horrendous emotional events that happen, either: the days of nonstop crying (both yours and the baby's), the colic and teething nightmares, and the number of miles you've walked around the dining room table in the middle of the night. I would advise that you wait until your postpartum depression has subsided before you write any entries at all.

Mostly the baby book is a place where you write things, beginning with a brief, sanitized description of labor, delivery, and the first few days of life. (Obviously you're going to want to leave out the part when you threatened to bite the labor nurse if she didn't get those ice chips right then.) Then you make a list of all the people who came to visit and brought layettes; and then, later on, you're supposed to keep track of the kid's important dates, such as when he got his first tooth, said his first word, and swallowed a mouthful of chopped carrots without spitting them at you.

While a baby book is designed to be written on a day-by-day basis, be aware that you're not the only person in the world who's going to write it after the fact—sometimes well after the fact. One of my mother's friends kept a baby book for her fourth child that read: "1964 or 1965 through approx. 1982: Mikey was born, drooled a lot as a baby, played soccer in second grade, and graduated with honors."

Faking the Baby Book

It's possible to wait too long to write the baby book, and then—well, you'll have to make stuff up. Inventing a babyhood for your kid is not as easy as you may think, so here are some suggestions, in case your kid is about to graduate from high school and wants to know the facts:

- Labor lasted four hours and was marked with excitement and euphoria that our darling baby was about to be born. I did crossword puzzles and chatted with the labor nurses, who were very sweet, while (insert husband's name here) kept an eye on the baby monitor and practiced his golf swing. When it was time for the birth, the doctor/midwife/labor nurse said he/she had never seen a more beautiful, intelligent, alert, responsive baby (choose one, or feel free to use all four, especially if you were knocked out by anesthesia at that point), and asked if we might pose for a TV commercial for the newborn unit. We declined; our family's privacy is too precious to us.
- Early visitors: List everyone you ever heard of. No doubt they really were there.
- Gifts: The word layette is all you need.
- First days: Use phrases like "bursting with pride," "sleeps through the night," and "already smiling."

- First tooth: Four months old is always a safe bet.
- First word: "Dada." (They all say "Dada" first.)
- First steps: If you feel your child was an athletic prodigy, you might go as low as seven months. Any younger than that will arouse distrust later on and put the entire baby book under a cloud of suspicion. If your baby was just average, lie anyway and say eleven months.
- Toilet training: Leave this out completely.

Toys, or—as some people think of them—infant intelligence enhancers

You might as well know that many people these days are thinking you should be "maximizing your baby's potential." They want to know what tricks you are teaching your kid, and what educational materials you are using. Let me just tell you right now that patty-cake and peek-a-boo, which used to be the cutting edge of baby scholarship, no longer mean squat. This is because somehow our nation has gotten an inferiority complex after realizing that children in other countries know how to run government surveillance units while our kids are still watching Barney and Baby Bop. This has made some of our patriotic citizens a little cranky, and naturally they are busy thinking up ways to get our current babies intellectually enhanced—so that soon American toddlers can be setting up surveillance units along with the other international babies.

It used to be that a baby could just play with a couple of wooden blocks, and no one would think a thing about it. But lately it seems a kid waving around two blocks in the air is "working on her hand-eye coordination" or "enhancing the large motor skills." (Those, in case you're wondering, are what then enable the baby to throw the blocks at your head. Hand-eye coordination determines if it actually hits you.)

Some people start while the baby is still in the womb, using speakerphones to play language tapes and other educational materials designed for fetal enhancement. But I didn't go in for all that stuff, because I figured that the act of growing arms and legs was probably taxing enough on a baby, and that after a long day working on neurons, a kid shouldn't be expected to listen to geography tapes.

Still, I'm all for babies being intelligent, so I did talk to them before they were born. I said things like, "If you kick my pancreas one more time, there is going to be hell to pay when you get born." And when one of them was bordering on being two weeks overdue, in the middle of the hottest summer the Northeast has ever seen, I said, "I want you to know that it's safe to come out, because we just bought an air conditioner for your room."

My friend Ellie, however, really fell for the potential-maximizing concept in a big way. Right after her son was born, she went out and bought special optically stimulating mobiles and flash cards, as well as textbooks-on-tape for those long, empty afternoons when a newborn doesn't have much else to occupy his time. She also spelled things in his presence—like, "Now I'm going to change your diaper. D-I-A-P-E-R. And after that, you can eat. E-A-T. But please no more poops for a while. P-O-O-P-S."

We, her friends, had to admit that her kid did probably have the highest newborn IQ on the block—but, at twelve months, he was eating houseflies and crawling backwards, just the same as all the rest of the babies we knew. So what that he'd had a 42 Presidents flash card series game since he was two days old and had heard that James was the most common name for an American president? It didn't help him one bit when he got to be a toddler and had to negotiate for trucks in the sandbox. One time I heard another two-year-old scream, "You poophead!" at him, and I waited, holding my breath, to see if he was going to respond with,

70

"Well, you're a P-O-O-P head!" But he just cried. That kind of early knowledge doesn't last, I guess.

And neither do any of those well-meaning baby toys, I'm afraid. There's some disappointing news in store for you about toys, if you're thinking of buying any, which of course, you have to. People will give you dirty looks if your child's room isn't stocked up with age-appropriate baby toys. But here's the truth about toys: You go out and buy the nicest stuffed animal you can find for your child, and when she unwraps the box, the thing that catches her eye is the four-color brochure the company tucked inside. This is what your kid becomes attached to—and screams for during the times it's hiding out under the couch.

Our American factories are laboring day and night to come up with fun, educational toys that can help our country get ahead in the world, and no one can bear to tell them that it's pretty much their brochures that are the big hits with kids.

We once went through an entire summer where our two-year-old's favorite toy wasn't a toy at all: It was the M-Z section of the Spanish-English dictionary. I would have been proud at how intellectually advanced this made us look— handing out a dictionary to the baby, after all—except that it was such an incredible feat of survival to keep track of the damn thing. Every day I had to search up and down for its various pages, which were always coming unglued and fluttering off behind radiators and underneath the car seats, or being chewed up in little wads by the kid. For nearly three months, we never got anywhere on time because pages 145-150, which were deemed by the baby to be the all-time best ones, kept getting lost.

Then, before I could even make it to the park to brag to my Mama Friends about how attached our toddler was to the foreign language dictionary, one day an advertising supplement for aluminum siding arrived at our house—and the dictionary pieces were forgotten forever. I'm sorry, but no one is willing to be impressed by your kid needing to cuddle an aluminum siding photo.

The other stuff that really makes young children happy—and that it is your job to discourage them from using—is anything made of glassware, toxic substances, or iron. Infants especially love iron products. I've seen them crawl on a sticky kitchen floor at speeds approaching 30 mph to get to the cabinet where the iron skillet is located, just so they can lug it out and try to bang themselves on the foot with it.

It is one of my proudest accomplishments in life that I once got my nine-month-old to play with an empty coffee can merely by acting as if it were a dangerous, heavy object that could seriously injure a baby. I kept looking at it worriedly and then putting it down—and then coming back to it with deep concern furrowed on my face. By the time I relinquished it, the baby was so wild for it that she played with it, nonstop, for the rest of the year. She stared at the reflection of herself in the shiny bottom of the can; she rolled it across the room while making motor noises; she put things into it and then emptied them out. It was the perfect, all-purpose toy.

I've often thought this could be a helpful hint to the toy manufacturers. Maybe they could present their toys in packages that said: "Don't let babies near this very horrible product. Only the brochure itself is safe for a person under the age of 21." No baby could resist that.

All-Time Favorite Toys

- The toilet brush
- Lids from pots and pans, the heavier the better
- Anything in your cosmetics drawer
- The family's toothbrushes
- Fireplace tools
- Your keys

Light cords, outlets, stove knobs:
A cover for everything

Once your baby gets to be about six months old, you are going to fall on your knees and thank God that you are bringing a child in the world in the modern age when you can find something to cover up every dangerous thing in the world. I don't know what the Cro-Magnon parents must have done, what with bison teeth and igneous rocks lying all over the camp and no little plastic caps to shield a baby from their sharp edges.

The hard part of being a modern parent is trying to convince everyone else that the world is a hideously dangerous place for little human beings and that they should join you in your protection efforts. Your main job for a while is going to be to try to convince everyone you know to invest in enough plastic covers so that you can take just a couple of worry-free blinks in your life. My friend Jackie solved this by carrying spare outlet covers in her purse for years—and whenever she'd go visit anyone, she'd spend the first twenty minutes crawling around under their tables and chairs, plugging their electrical outlets with little plastic covers. This, you see, is the kind of neurosis Cro-Magnons didn't have to deal with.

But outlet covers, you'll find, are just the least of it. What I couldn't stand was the way all tables seemed to be designed to be the exact height of a baby's eyeball. I mean, is this a conspiracy against small children, or what? There were whole years of my life when I was forever throwing my body between babies and table corners, which made conversation with other adults disjointed and unsatisfactory. I'd be at my friend Sue's house, hearing about her new boyfriend, when suddenly one of my kids would toddle within ten feet of the coffee table, and I'd say, "Sorry, Sue," and do a combination leap/slide maneuver, rather like a baseball player making it into home plate.

Luckily, there are huge corporations now specifically committed to creating little plastic devices to help with this. Besides covers for the electrical outlets, there are also soft corners to put on tables and covers for the knobs on the stove so that the baby can't pull a chair over and turn on all the burners at once and catch his diaper on fire. There are latches for the cabinets, so that he can't drink up all the cleaning products under the sink, or play with the iron skillet when you're not watching. There are covers for all the faucets, for the dog's food dish, and for electrical outlets that already have something plugged into them so the baby can't pull the plug out with his wet little hand and get himself electrocuted. There are prison-quality baby gates for stairways and doorways and fences that you can put around your house-plants.

Actually, in this day and age, there is no danger that cannot be somehow guarded, covered, or protected against a baby.

But the sad thing is that, even with all these protections, you still will not get your fair share of blinks until your child reaches the Age of Common Sense and Reason, which for many of them is once they have already left home and have jobs—long after you've developed nervous tics and have had to go on medication.

This is because a fair number of babies are born knowing how to remove the outlet covers and cabinet latches, and even though they politely conceal this from you, knowing how bad it will make you feel that your work has been in vain, one day you will look up and your fifteen-month-old will be handing you the oven cleaner. If he could talk, he would say, "Here. I probably shouldn't be playing with this, since it's pretty dangerous. You might want to put it where I can't get to it again."

Truly creative babies can think of many more ways to get hurt than American corporations can figure ways to stop them. Just walking across the room can be hazardous to their health. You'll be watching, when all of a sudden a baby will—for no discernible reason—fall down backwards and land on his head. Unless you're willing to consign yourself to living in a completely padded world (which my friend Liz did, but she had eleven-month-old twin boys, and it was either pad the house or have a nervous breakdown), you are going to witness an unbelievable number of scrapes and bruises and near misses.

Some days the only comfort at all is the knowledge that the human race has somehow made it for a long, long time—and that when the kid goes to sleep, you can have a glass of scotch. That's something the Cro-Magnons didn't have.

The sex lives of paraphernalia

There's another kind of stuff that collects in your house when you have a little one, you know. It's not just the strollers and playpens and hand-eye coordination toys that start proliferating. You could handle that stuff—even the changing tables and the receiving blankets and the sitting-backwards car seats. What's way worse than all of that stuff is the unbelievable amount of little tiny parts of things that begin to accumulate along your baseboards, between the couch cushions, and under the refrigerator.

Legos. Wheels to tiny little cars. Superballs. Arms of former action figures. Barbie's dinner plates. (Did you know Barbie had a need for dinner plates?) Bows that the stuffed animals once wore. Magnetic letters of the alphabet. Doll hairbrushes.

Beaded bracelets. Tiny little people dressed in Native American costumes.

Your purse, too, will start to fill up with these things. One day you'll reach in for your checkbook, and the best you'll be able to come up with is the top to the Tommy Tippee cup, one Lincoln log, and a broken green crayon. Where you once kept your wallet is now a baby doll's bottle and the insides to a plastic toy camera. And, at night, climbing into bed, you'll find a wad of Play-Doh under your pillow and Barbie's evening gown tangled up with the blankets.

No one knows for sure where all this stuff comes from, or why it pursues people with children so relentlessly. Until you have kids, you're pretty well able to fight off junk, but once reproduction has taken place in your house, everything around you suddenly also has a sex life. You've obviously sent some sort of signal that it's okay to indulge.

Caps to markers, which were once sterile and politely went to their doom in the trash can without argument, now make their way to freedom behind the stove, where they reproduce like mad. You will come into the kitchen one morning, and marker caps will be in every drawer you open, behind the cereal bowls, and scattered throughout the dishwasher.

Some people have households in which coat hangers reproduce, but I have never had much success with those. My coat hangers are quite elderly, I believe, since rather than reproducing, many of them seem to be dropping dead in the closet and being disposed of quietly by the others.

But just let your family visit a fast-food restaurant and buy a children's meal, and let me tell you, within a week the little plastic toy that was slipped into the kid's bag has become three thousand plastic toys. My theory is that these things ride around in your warm car, where they slip behind the seats and reproduce, making lots of other plastic thingies, and then they jump in your purse and infiltrate your house. Their plan is to someday take over the world, and they realize that the best way is through toddlers.

I have gone on major plastic purges in my house, where my only goal was to be able to walk through a room without stepping on some miniature device—and within twenty-four hours, I've noticed, it all comes back again, sometimes bringing friends along.

Chapter 5:
Postcard from Your Marriage

The guy across the pillow— old what's-his-name

There is no end to the number of people who want to tell you that your marriage is going to be transformed once you get a child.

Trust me: They don't mean this in a nice way. You can tell by the way they're doubled over, laughing, and with tears in their eyes, they're saying, "Oooh hoo, I can't picture you figuring out how to get a baby to go to sleep, or changing all those billions of diapers! And the sex! Hoo boy, are the two of you ever going to miss all that! You're never going to feel like having sex again—just kiss it good-bye!"

Well, I just want to tell you that there is sex after babies—that's how people get more than one kid. As for the diapers—there aren't really a billion of them. Probably just a couple million, and you'll share some of those. And who needs sleep, really? Besides, having a baby brings your marriage to a whole new level of things to talk about.

For instance, there's what-did-you-say-your-name-was-again discussion, which is very popular for the first few months after a baby is born, a time when some of your brain cells seem to have left your body right along with the baby. No matter how well you thought you knew each other's names before the birth, it seems that that particular file gets misplaced in the brain reorganization that takes place when you first become a parent.

This makes perfect sense when you stop and think about it. After all, your brain, which was already filled to overflowing with useless facts you'll never need again—like the fact that William Howard Taft was the first golfer to become president—now has to let some information go so that it can remember, for instance, not to leave the baby's car seat (with baby inside) on the hood of the car when you drive away. But every now and then, instead of letting go of the useless facts about the presidents, it deletes the Fact File on things like your mate's name, birth date, and his official opinion on the Coke vs. Pepsi question.

Mind you, this is not stuff that's totally eliminated forever. It's just misplaced for the time being. Maybe you're going to discover that your husband's birth date has been moved to the same folder that contains multiplication tables 1-5, and so the brain has to do a little extra work to locate it. My friend Cathy once called her husband the baby's name, then their dog's name, then the name of their town ("Hey, Springfield!") before lighting on her old boyfriend's name and being stunned that he didn't answer. By that time he was miffed. He said if there was going to be a shortage of brain real estate, then he didn't see that the old boyfriend deserved any of the neurons that were left behind.

It may help if you simply start referring to everyone around you as "honey" or "sweetheart." I have never much liked those words, but I think they must have been invented by people who had just given birth and had temporarily misplaced the Family Members' Names File.

Missing objects

For reasons that no one knows for sure, the birth of a baby can cause many objects to get lost. You may have spent your entire marriage being secure in the fact that you knew where things went: spoons in the kitchen drawer, important papers in the file marked Important Papers, and your paycheck on the desk next to the telephone until you take it to the bank.

Forget about all that. It's a whole new ball game, as far as household objects are concerned.

My theory—and frankly I can't get anyone else to back this up—is that objects see the opportunity of a new baby in the house as a time to make their move. After all, things are stirred up, and they feel that in the confusion they can make their escape. Because they have to do their worst during the times that you aren't looking at them, most of them can't really make it all the way out the front door and to freedom, so they do the next best thing: They hide out somewhere that they think you'd never look. A spoon, for example, will happily go to the bottom of the laundry hamper; the camera will go to visit the contact lens solution in the bathroom closest; the pair of pants you wore last week and want to wear again will be wadded up behind the bed.

You may be wondering what this has to do with your marriage. Well, you and your mate will spend a lot of time asking each other questions that begin with, "Have you seen...?" and "Where do you think...?" Be warned that you'll soon be saying, "For God's sake, I just put this down a few minutes ago! You must know what happened to it!"

It opens up a whole new facet of your relationship, actually. Looking for stuff together bonds you in a way that nothing else in courtship and early marriage could ever have done. And if you don't kill each other, that helps.

It gets even more interesting once your baby can move around. Babies have a knack for attracting lost objects; they're like Venus flytraps in this way. Your paycheck, for instance, the one that you're sure you put on the desk next to the telephone? It will one day decide to go off to play with the baby and, after being gummed for a while, it will go for rides in the secret compartment of his toy oil tanker, a compartment that you didn't even know existed.

Your birth certificate and marriage license are also willing to jump out of the Important Papers folder and make their way alone in the world. While you sleep, in fact, the entire folder is working its way, millimeter by millimeter, out of its file cabinet, and within a few months will be disgorging its contents to the four corners of the household and beyond.

Many of the things that get loose in the world will be eaten by the baby. Unfortunately, there's no way to alert objects to this possibility in advance, or perhaps more of them would stay where they belong. You can try going in and whispering over the file cabinet every few days or so, "We have a drooling monster out here who loves nothing more than shredding paper and then eating it!" But I don't know if it would really help. And if you're not careful, the baby monitor might pick up your words and broadcast them to the neighbors, and you may not want them to know you talk to objects.

The work question

As if the Lost Object Search and the I-mixed-up-your-name-with-the-name-of-our-town discussion aren't stimulating enough, there are even more new transformations awaiting the two of you. For one thing, it's now time to figure out an entirely new division of labor.

Even if you got all that taken care of in the first few months of marriage ("You do the dishes on Tuesdays and Thursdays, I do the laundry in months with no L?"), there is now so much more work to be divided up, and for the first few weeks, at least, it's important to spend more time talking about work than actually doing any. You don't want to start doing more of your share, and risk setting a precedent that's hard to get out of later.

My friend Barbara's husband thought he'd worked out the perfect solution when he said, "You change the baby, and I'll change the oil."

When Barbara pointed out that the baby would need to be changed many, many more times than the oil, he agreed to throw in changing the air conditioner filters each season, too. And, okay, he'd change the window screens to storm windows and then back again. Potentially, he said, this was going to give him quite a hectic Saturday sometime when all this needed to be done in one day. Therefore, he deserved to rest up the rest of the year.

Also, my friend Linda's husband decided that she could take care of the kid for the first nine years, and he'd take over during the last nine. He pointed out that since this meant he'd have to handle all the adolescent disputes, he was actually going to need to spend the first nine years working on his ferocious voice, so that he could deliver lines like, "I said you may not take my car!" in an impressive way.

This is exactly the reason that it's unwise to sign any binding work agreements in the first few months. Things that may sound as though they have some reason behind them are actually scams in disguise.

There are several key questions that will come up and need to be resolved:

- Is nursing considered work when technically all a woman has to do is lift up her shirt and allow the baby to latch onto her? This may involve the age-old discussion of Just What Is Work Anyway. If you use the restrictive definition that movement must take place and sweat get generated, then possibly nursing does not qualify. However, if work is defined as "anything that uses calories" (which I would recommend), then nursing is certainly a valid form of work.
- Are credits to be given, retroactively, for the work of carrying around the fetus, expertly conducting oxygen

and glucose into its little developing systems, and then spending an entire day giving birth to it? And if so, exactly how many loads of laundry would this be equal to?

- When counting up the numbers of diapers changed per person, should a poopy diaper count for more than simply a wet one?
- How many miles must you walk around the house with a screaming baby on your shoulder to get out of doing the dishes for one week?
- If a person should turn on the vacuum cleaner to quiet down a colicky baby, should that person be obligated also to vacuum the rug?
- If your mate is keeping the baby, and the baby sleeps the whole time, does that count for as much as if the baby screamed the entire time you were away? Some people think staying home with a sleeping baby is a lot like resting, not working at all, and should accrue no credits, but you have to find your own way here.

Above all, you don't want to get into the situation that my friend Marcy found herself in, where she was responsible for all the nursing and all the washing of dishes, and then she was expected to vacuum the rugs, too. She ended up having to devise a point system: Washing dishes was worth three points, changing poopy diapers varied from two to eight points (the maximum for a case of explosive diarrhea), and looking for lost objects was worth about six points, depending on how long it took to find stuff. She made a big chart and posted it in the kitchen—and at the end of the week, it was obvious to both her and her husband who had done the most work and who had some points to make up.

I probably don't have to tell you that this system just invites abuses. For one thing, she soon started to suspect her husband of actually hiding objects, just so he could claim they were lost and then get points for pretending to look for them. He would also declare that each diaper he changed had been of the high-point, disgusting caliber, which sometimes necessitated a trip to the diaper pail to have a husband-and-wife diaper-rating session.

This, Marcy said later, led their marriage into deeper, richer, uncharted territory than she had ever imagined they would reach in a lifetime of being together.

"When you see yourself standing over a diaper pail and measuring which diapers there are the worst, and who had to change the very worst ones—well, then I think it's time you step back and realize you have really bonded with this man," she said. "There's not another human being in the world you would have that conversation with."

Can you have a big night out, even at the grocery store?

Hardly anybody remembers how to go out on a date once they have a baby. I think this fact should be in wider circulation, because it's so depressing when you finally do go out with each other and discover that there's nothing the two of you want to do except perhaps go to the grocery store.

Your friends will all make fun of you if you admit that you finally hired a baby-sitter and only went to the supermarket before you came back home, but let me tell you; there are those of us who understand that there's a lot of joy to be had in doing the grocery shopping without a small child with you; lingering over the produce without worrying that a certain ten-pounder is going to wake up and start accusing you of mistreatment, right in front of the other customers. It's not easy to look for food for the week when you're also having to pat a baby, sing "Toora Loora Loora," or, worse, stop and breast-feed, right there in the store. (You'd think the dairy section would be the best place to nurse, but really, there is no good place. The dairy section is far too cold, and there aren't any seats. You're better off in the lawn-chair section.)

The laundromat is another really good place for a date, although underrated by childless people. You can read or talk in there without too many interruptions, and at least until the clothes are finished, there's not much else you have to do but relax, which is more than you can say for those places you might go to dance.

An even greater benefit to going to the laundromat on a date is that you might even be able to catch a little nap, listening to the soothing sounds of the washers and dryers.

Just take my advice and don't tell anybody where you went.

The difference between a mom and a dad

Even though the two of you attended the same birth and came home from the hospital with the same baby, you're most likely going to find there are some major reactions you don't have in common. Like nothing else on earth—with the possible exception of facial hair shaving—having a baby really does emphasize the differences between the sexes.

For instance, a woman who has just had a baby remembers every detail of the whole experience. For months, she tells the story of labor and delivery to everyone who can't get away from her fast enough, and even years later, she can recall the precise inflection of the doctor's voice when he said, "Time to push!"

A guy remembers that the hospital personnel kept nagging him about moving his car—and that when the baby finally came out, somebody handed him a pair of scissors and said, "Cut this thing here," meaning the umbilical cord.

Another thing: Even though a man and a woman were about equal in knowledge when she first got pregnant, now she throws around words like colostrum, episiotomy, and Apgar score as though they were regular English words in wide usage, while he has to consult a glossary to know the difference between onesies and umbilical stumps. Not only that, but she can tell you the day the baby first smiled and what he's worn every day since birth, and give you a detailed rundown on what the different cries mean. She's become a Professor of Childbirth and Babyhood.

He loves the baby and all that, but he'd be hard-pressed to list Five Baby Events Since Birth. This is not due to any lack of emotional depth in men, as some women believe. It's simply that because of irrefutable biological laws, he didn't get to grow a new person in his own private body, he still has his pre-pregnancy weight, and no one is living off the fluids his body knows how to make and spurt out.

But the major difference between new fathers and mothers is that, chances are, he remembers what it was like to have a sex life. And because he didn't just get finished pushing the equivalent of a large rib roast out of his body, he's probably thinking it would be fun to have one again—a sex life, that is. Oh, he'd probably go for a rib roast as well, if someone were willing to cook him one. But for a while, at least, most systems are shut down: cooking, sex, housekeeping—even talking without crying. He can't believe the amount of crying that's now in his life.

Let's face it: If you were going to characterize life with a new baby, chances are the word moist would be in the top five adjectives. There is, in fact, a whole sea of fluids being manufactured, moment by moment. And none of them belongs to the father. This is a time when many guys start calling home first before leaving work. "Uh, what's the humidity level around there? Do we have milk and tears going? Do we need a mop-up crew?"

A woman, after spending most of her days in such damp proximity to a baby—both of them oozing from all orifices—is hardly going to think that what she's been missing in life is a chance to have sex. I'm sorry, but that's just the way it is. Sex is something people think of when they're pretty much dried off and when somebody's mouth isn't chewing on them for forty-five minutes out of every hour, day after day.

Sex is also best when neither one of the partners is crying because of a poignant long-distance commercial that was on television earlier in the day.

This doesn't last forever, of course. One night, just as the guy is getting used to a lifetime of celibacy (after all, the baby's already six weeks old and there's been no action yet), she'll turn to him across the pillow and give him their old familiar sign.

His heart leaps up. *She wants me!* sings through his cells. He reaches for her across the blankets—so what if they're a little damp from when the baby was in their bed earlier? Life is gloriously messy and damp! Sex is gloriously messy and damp!

But then, naturally, the baby cries.

Babies, through some kind of sophisticated neurological tracking system, are always aware when their parents are undertaking any sort of sexual activity. For some really sensitive babies, all it takes is a smile across a mound of dirty dishes. And there have been reported cases of babies waking up when their parents were two states away and had merely thought about stopping in a motel. But most babies are willing to let things get to the touching stage before they insist on waking up and becoming part of the action.

No one knows quite why this mechanism works so well. It could be that the subtle changes in air currents when parents reach for each other is enough to jolt a baby into awakening. Still others say that babies simply are pleasure-seekers and want to join in on the fun.

But I think it's just that babies want to be in on any decisions having to do with other babies coming into the family. They wake up, basically, so they can protect their turf. If they could talk, they'd be saying, "That's my uterus! You eggs and sperm will not get together in there!"

Go ahead: Think up other places to have sex. Go out to the car, head for the kitchen—anywhere you think the baby won't be disturbed, should it happen that one of you makes the slightest sound of pleasure. It won't matter. The baby is wired to wake up. There will be lots of times that you find yourselves trying to make love under deadline conditions, while your baby hollers at you from the confines of the bassinet.

My friend Ted once yelled over to his newborn son, "It's okay. We're using precautions. You won't have a sibling for some time yet!"

I wish I could say that this was enough to reassure the baby, and he went back to sleep. But babies—many of whom were born holding "precautions" in their little fists—know better than to trust such things.

Chapter 6:
A Bunch of New Things to Worry About in the Middle of the Night

- Crib death.
- Projectile vomiting.
- Choking.
- Car wrecks, airplane crashes, major fires, trees falling on the house during a windstorm.
- The one glass of wine you had during pregnancy will turn out to have been consumed the week the part of his brain was forming that has to do with becoming a good person, and he'll be a menace to society.
- He'll roll off the changing table, even though you are standing right there, but one day you'll look away for one second and that's when it will happen.
- The smoke detectors might not be working just right, and it's too late to buy batteries tonight so you're just going to have to stay awake and sniff for fires until morning.
- His first word will be shit.
- The babysitter you hired is really having parties with sailors while you are at work each day.
- You are always going to cry during long-distance commercials on television.

89

- The baby's hat will slide down over his nose, suffocating him while you are out walking with him in the stroller and you won't notice in time.
- Your neighbors heard you discussing their marriage in the baby monitor.
- The first time he ever climbs out of his crib, you won't realize that he knows how, and he'll get all the way down the stairs and out the front door before you know he's gone.
- You will never find a bathing suit that fits you again.
- All those people who told Ann Landers they wished they'd never had kids were on to something that you'll figure out soon.
- The fact that he likes the baby swing so much means that he's going to grow up to be a race car driver or attempt to climb Mount Everest, and he'll have no regard for your feelings on the subject whatsoever.
- You have already forgotten the Heimlich maneuver for babies.
- You have the patience of a gnat.
- He'll always have those reddish birthmarks on his eyelids.
- All the other babies in the park will always ignore him.
- His car seat will come unhinged, and when you hit the brakes, he'll go flying out the window.
- One day he will drool sooo much that when you go to pick him up, he'll slip right out of your arms and land on the floor.
- You will never find enough money for college in eighteen years, by which time they are predicting it will cost about one million dollars per year.
- Those little hook-on-the-edge-of-the-table high chair seats in restaurants, which work by magic anyway, will one day simply start responding to the pull of

gravity like everything else on earth, and it will be while your baby is strapped into one.

- He'll be one of those men who tells women, "I'll call you," and then never does—and women all over the city will decide you, as the mother, taught him wrong.
- You still haven't figured out where you stand on Santa Claus, the Easter bunny, and the tooth fairy.
- He'll put out his eye with the sharp edge of a cookie.
- He's not having the correct number of poops.
- Someone will see you trying to get him to burp and call the child abuse hot line because you're banging him on the back.
- He won't learn how to laugh.
- In seventh grade, he won't get picked for the baseball team, which he wants above everything else, and you'll have to persuade him that it doesn't really matter or else you'll have to go beat up the coach.
- You'll ask the pediatrician a question so stupid that you'll be labeled Neurotic Parent, and it will say so in red letters on the front of your child's chart, and no question you ask again will be taken seriously.
- You are shallow and vain to care about the fact that all your dry-cleanable clothes have spit-up on the shoulders.
- You've already forgotten the difference between onesies and zwieback.
- He won't go to the prom.
- You'll forget that you put him in his car seat on the hood of your car and will drive away, the way you did that day with your Coke.
- He'll always be two months behind on the Baby Skills Checklist.
- He may have the sarcasm gene, like your brother.

Chapter 7: Sleep and Other Lies

Sleep as a recreational goal

I had hardly had a new baby for two weeks when it hit me that I was never again going to be rested. Well, maybe not never. I had some wisp of hope that perhaps when the kid went off to college, I'd get a full night's sleep again. I could sure as hell see it wasn't going to be during his infancy. And God knows that toddlerhood (when, after all, he'd know how to actually get around on his own) didn't seem likely, nor did the school years—especially the high school years, when he'd no doubt either be playing electric guitar in his bedroom, or else he'd be out driving around in fast, dangerous cars. One day, as I sat for a stuporous ten minutes trying to figure out whether the sock I was holding was a left sock or a right sock, it hit me: My best hope was that he'd get into a residential college someday, and I'd have huge chunks of time when I'd be allowed to get a full component of sleep.

This, I don't have to tell you, is not much of a comfort when you're staring down at somebody who weighs seven pounds, and who hasn't even registered for the SATs yet.

I could see that for years I was going to be so tired that yawns and sighs would take the place of real words in my vocabulary. I was going to be saying phrases like, "You know, hand me the thing," all because I didn't have the necessary wattage for a full brain search and retrieval. I could see that yawning was going to be big, really big. You just can feel this in your bones, insofar as you can feel anything except raw, strung-out fatigue. It's tough to admit that this seven-pounder is holding most of your brain power hostage, but the fact is, every time you manage to lapse into something resembling sleep, he wakes up and wants to resume wide-awake life in your presence.

"He likes you," said our pediatrician once, when I attempted to explain that the baby was awake for twenty-three hours of every twenty-four. "He's probably going to grow into a very social person."

Pediatricians mean well, they really do, but surely I'm not the only one who suspects they learned some tricks in medical school that they're unwilling to share with the rest of us poor slobs who forgot to get our medical degrees before having children. Or maybe it's that although pediatricians' kids don't sleep any more than ours do, the doctors themselves don't mind, because being a resident in a hospital, getting ten minutes of sleep per week, ruthlessly prepared them for their years of parenthood. Whatever it is, many pediatricians are almost unfailingly cheerful when you tell them the baby doesn't sleep, as though this is just another sign that you have delivered a very interesting and delightful baby.

Once I told our doctor that I was putting all my hopes in the fact that our six-week-old baby would someday go off to college and that I would catch up on my sleep during his freshman year. He gave me a doctorly little smile and suggested that often it was possible to get a little rest when the baby is napping during the day.

"Which nap would that be?" I said. "The one from ten-thirty until ten-thirty-eight, or perhaps the second nap, from two-twenty to two-fifty?"

"That last one sounds more promising," he said, in perfect seriousness. "But maybe, under the circumstances, you could try for both."

I never thought striving for sleep was a lofty-enough ambition in life, but I came to see otherwise. Parenthood makes you realize that small goals are perhaps best: Instead of wanting to solve the world's hunger crisis, or get to work on time five days in a row, for instance, there were huge periods in my life when I thought I deserved an award if I managed to get out of my bathrobe by, say, 2:15 P.M., when the mailman came. I also could be proud of myself if I managed, on three hours of sleep, to remember that I had last seen my car keys in the cat food dish. I didn't ask myself why the keys were there, or whether I had even been the one to put them there. I was contenting myself with small goals. Perhaps, I said to myself, by the time the kid is in nursery school for a few hours each day, I'll be able to question the deeper meanings of things.

In the meantime, I decided that there had to be a way to get the sleep I needed. I discovered that it was usually possible to doze while talking on the telephone, especially if I asked people to please speak softly. It's possible to get about twenty seconds of sleep during the typical telemarketing call, and the best part is that the telemarketer doesn't even want a response from you. She's so worried you're going to interrupt her and say some form of the word no that she'll be happy to unravel her entire spiel while you nap. You can just lean against the wall, close your eyes, and be off in dreamland before you hear the dial tone again.

Calls from relatives are a little harder, particularly if they expect you to tell them details about the baby. It's hard to make a snore sound like actual words, after all. But if you can remain awake long enough to tell them a couple of things, and then ask a leading question, like, "What do you think is wrong with the world's moral situation today, as it relates to the Middle East?" then you have a shot of getting

94

up to a good forty-five minutes of deep, refreshing sleep, with no more than an occasional "Hmmm" being required of you. (If your particular relative is too excitable on the subject of the Middle East, you might want to ask a more boring question, such as, "What meals have you eaten in the past three weeks for breakfast, lunch, and dinner, and how have you liked each of them?")

You definitely have to think creatively when it comes to grabbing an extra few naps here and there. Just remember that no nap is too small to do you some bit of good. You can close your eyes while you're stopped at a red light, assured that the very nanosecond the light turns to green, the driver behind you will be happy to let you know. And if you've memorized the placement of all your teeth, you may be able to grab a quick nap while brushing them if you can lean your head against the mirror.

And don't overlook grocery shopping. Store managers are used to people standing immobile for long periods, staring stupidly at fifteen kinds of corn flakes, so chances are they won't bother you if you prop yourself against the cart and doze off. Just make sure the wheels are lodged against some immovable object; you don't want to wake up to find yourself sailing into the meat locker.)

Even the simple activity of blinking shouldn't be overlooked as a possibility; in time you can train yourself to rest during those longer blinks. After all, if the baby can get by on just five minutes of sleep every now and then, you should be able to also. The trick is to turn no opportunity away.

Get over the sanctity of the marriage-bed thing

Okay, so once you liked the idea of satin sheets, thick white down comforters, piles of feather pillows with embroidery on them. And once upon a time you saw your bed as symbolic of everything that was right about your marriage, and your life. It was your sanctuary, your place of sexual abandon, your hideout from the world.

Well, maybe it wasn't that good, but it certainly wasn't this puddle you find yourself sleeping in now that there's an infant in it.

Some people will argue that babies have no place in their parents' beds—not now, not ever. But I think most of those people arguing this position don't have children. The ones with kids are way too tired to argue. I say, if it means being able to get a bit more sleep, allow anything into your bed that you have to. As a woman who has spent many, many nights in a double bed populated by a grown man, two cats, a baby, and a three-year-old who brought along his Tonka backhoe and a jack-o'-lantern, I certainly can't criticize anything other people might permit to join them in bed, unless, of course, livestock is involved, and even then I'd have to hear the whole story before I could make a judgment.

It's not just that babies think that the middle of the night is a great time for several of their meals, either, although that does go on for quite a long while. Long after the two, four, and six A.M. feedings are a thing of the past, most babies are still ordering their parents around in the middle of the night for no discernible reason other than that they know they can.

They've also got this hang-up about being mammals. I know you probably didn't tell them yet about their mammalian heritage, but they got the news just the same, in the Uterus University they attended while you were lugging them around for nine months. The average baby definitely feels that, as a mammal, she has a permanent nesting place in her parents' bed, and that she is entitled to as much animal contact as she can get for herself during every twenty-four-hour period. In utero, somehow they get the idea that you're going to let them hang onto your body at all times, and for a long while afterwards (until they're about twelve years old, actually) they act as though you've broken some sacred contract with them if you see it otherwise. The whole idea that everybody has his own special sleeping place and that we humans actually relish our time of restful solitude is a difficult concept to get across, no matter how many times you bring it up with them.

So, after you try the usual techniques the advice books give you—let the baby cry, then go in and pat her briefly up to a hundred times a night—you will probably end up doing what a sizable percentage of parents do: hauling the baby back to your own bed and informing her in your firmest voice that all of you intend to get some more sleep, whether any of you are snacking or not.

This would be great if not for a few details. For one thing, the baby obviously has to go in the center position, between you and your husband, because otherwise the little rascal will do her famous rollover trick right off the side of your bed, which will not do.

So you put the baby in the middle and carefully stack all the pillows so that they won't fall down on top of her face and smother her. You whisper to your husband that he shouldn't roll over at all for the next few hours, that he is to sleep in exactly the same position he is now in.

He says, "Mmmmph. Ghumpfh, fraghuts," which probably means that he agrees and is willing to do this.

You settle the baby in the crook of your arm and close your eyes. The baby nurses for a while—nice, slow, rhythmic nursing—and you slip back to sleep, grateful for this moment, God, so grateful. Not only do you have this perfect baby and perfect husband (who, after all, is willing to sleep in one position for the rest of the night), but you have so brilliantly managed your life and your safe method of pillow stacking that you are now going to get at least another four hours of sleep. Four hours seems like an absolute eternity. You can pay off a huge chunk of your sleep debt with four hours. And tomorrow, you will probably be able to speak in complete sentences without wanting to nap during the "uhhhs."

You drift off with all these soft little sounds in your head: the baby's suckling noises, your husband's low snoring as his vertebrae harden into position, your own nerve endings in your arm starting to scream out in protest against the weight of the baby crushing them. But you can sleep through all that, easily.

It's hard to say when it dawns on you that you're sleeping in a puddle, that your husband has left the bed (you later discover him calling chiropractors on the kitchen phone), and also that the baby has managed to work herself into a position where her legs and feet are kicking your internal organs with great velocity and intensity. The stack of pillows has fallen down over your face, and when you push them aside, you see by the clock that it's seven-thirty. A decent hour!

So what that you're soaked, and that your husband has to seek medical manipulation so he can walk upright? You got some sleep, didn't you?

The infants' theory of sleep

Just like the rest of us, babies have a lot of theories. They have their notions of how life is supposed to go, based on stuff they heard while they were still in gamete form, or else information they've gathered in their short lives as air-breathers. They are always on the lookout for evidence to support their theories, too. You'll see them sometimes gazing off into the distance, frowning slightly. Some people will tell you that expression has more to do with what's going on inside their colons, but I think it's the same look you'll see on the face of a CEO about to institute a major policy change. Theories are being put into action.

Sleep is one of the main things new babies know a lot about. For the first three days of life, babies seem very excited about the idea of sleeping. Oh, sure, they hang out with you a little while after being born, just to check out the astonishing news that you're the face that goes with the voice they've been hearing for nine months, but then they can't think of much else they've wanted to see, and besides that, getting born was hard work, so they conk out.

All through the ensuing three days when you're introducing them to their relatives and your junior high school soccer coach and all the rest of the people who happen to traipse through your house, they open one eye sometimes, give a few grunts, and then lapse back into their basic default setting, which is sleep.

There will be whole days when you are standing around, glancing at your watch, saying, "Which month do the books say this kid will actually wake up and do something?" Watch out if you say this around other parents; they will all tell you trite, ridiculous stuff about how you should count your blessings.

But then it ends.

Maybe, deep inside their little infant brains, something has tipped them off that they're humans, and that the future lies in figuring out what's happening on planet earth. It is as though some switch has been turned on, and they're hit with the realization that they'd better get themselves organized. After all, there are only eighty or so years to try to understand astrophysics, the world banking system, and how electricity gets into the walls. Even babies know that with that kind of deadline, they can't waste time with a twenty-three-hour-a-day nap.

There is something reassuring about a baby suddenly turning curious this way. But, after you're reassured that yes, you really did give birth to a human being with a working brain, you have another huge adjustment to make. Suddenly you're in charge of a wide-awake newborn, who hangs around all the time, expecting vast amounts of unspecified entertainment.

This would be good if they thought watching you talk on the phone was entertaining. Or even if they liked *Murphy Brown* or old *thirty something* reruns. The trouble is that besides food and an occasional burp, there's not much going on that amuses them. They may think they want to get started on the astrophysics lectures, but frankly, they have enough difficulty remembering to hold their little jaws clamped around the nipple of the pacifier. The damn thing is therefore constantly falling on the floor, which enrages them ("This," you can say, "is your first lesson in gravity"), but the worst of it is that you then have to pick it up and go off to wash it, which they consider to be the unspeakable crime of desertion.

Once I called my friend Kate to report on my day with a five-week-old. "She nursed thirty-five times over an eight-hour period, and I picked up the pacifier and washed it a hundred and sixty-three times. And she cried whenever she couldn't think of anything else worth doing."

"Time," said Kate, "hangs heavy on a newborn's hands."

So they do the newborn equivalent of whining. They inflict damage on themselves by waving their fists in the air and bonking themselves on the head or scratching their own faces. They kick and fuss and complain. They holler in shrill, unpleasant voices that make you wistful for the sound of fingernails scraping down a blackboard somewhere.

They look as though they would love to go to sleep, if only someone could give them the map and explain to them the clear directions of how it is that you get there. But for the longest time, it seems that unless sleep sneaks up on them, bangs them over the head, and carts them off, they have no idea how to get themselves to drift off. And since they don't speak English, it's useless to keep saying to them over and over, "Just stop wailing and close your little eyes and wait for a few minutes!"

You might as well know that you are not the first desperate person to try to think up new and innovative ways

100

to convince a baby to go to sleep. There's a reason, you know, that the roads are full of cars in the middle of the night. These are all people with babies, driving around and hoping that something—the motion of the car, the grinding of the gears, the hint of carbon monoxide fumes—will eventually cause the baby to fall asleep. This works wonders, until you get home again. And unfortunately, you always do have to go home again.

Some friends of mine claim that dryers can help babies sleep. They set their wretchedly crying babies up in baby carriers next to the dryer, and then, I presume, they turn on the dryer and run out of the room. I have never known for sure how this works, unless babies are comforted by the idea that their laundry is being done. Maybe they're so stunned to find themselves consigned to the laundry room rather than in their customary cages that they finally just hush.

Still other people buy into the theory that if you just let babies cry it out, eventually they get so exhausted that they just fall asleep on their own. I have never personally seen this work. I have embarked on program after program in which I would decide to let the baby cry to exhaustion, only to realize that there are babies in the world (mine, for instance) who are quite capable of crying for the rest of their lives without once having the notion of sleep occur to them. Instead, they work on perfecting the Art of Crying until it can no longer technically be called crying. It resembles more a tropical hurricane. It was clear where we were heading—not for sleep, but for an explosion that would knock out the power in most of the neighborhood.

For a long time I thought I just wasn't doing it right. Either I must have misunderstood the rules of this put-the-baby-in-the-crib-and-let-it-cry method, or it was obviously a scam.

One day I cornered our pediatrician. "Tell me the truth," I said. "Is it guaranteed to always work, letting the baby cry herself to sleep? Does every baby eventually get there?"

He looked very uncomfortable.

"Well," he said, "actually, no. Some babies are so determined not to sleep that they will turn into atomic bombs, explode, knock out the power in your neighborhood for a week, and then you'll have pieces of screaming baby to pick up all over the room."

Okay, so that's not exactly what he said. I don't remember his exact words, but the gist of it was just that: Some babies will not agree to cry themselves to sleep.

But here's what he did say that helped a little: Nothing stays the way it is for very long. One week the baby won't sleep no matter what you do, and the next—just as you find yourself checking the want ads for Merchant Marine jobs and thinking up which doorstep you want to leave the kid on—you realize your baby has pretty much adapted to the human being schedule of sleeping in the night and mostly hanging out with you during the day.

And that must mean that your little baby is about to turn into a toddler.

The toddler view: Sleep as outrage

Toddlers technically need no sleep. They are actually tiny terrible robots that run on air particles that give them all the energy they need.

No, no. I'm only kidding. Actually, any reputable child development book will explain to you that the average toddler sleeps approximately twelve hours a day, which according to most calculations is a full half of the day. Since no one I know has ever had a toddler who did this, I think we can conclude that either there is no such thing as the "average" toddler, or else the day is not really twenty-four hours long.

It's obvious what's really going on here. Toddlers do probably sleep half the day, but they do it in one-minute-on-one-minute-off spurts. There are not enough consecutive minutes of sleep to allow you to even make your way to your own bed during their downtime. If you have this kind of toddler—and I think it's the standard-issue one—you had better train yourself to be able to drop and fall asleep in your tracks whenever the opportunity might present itself. Try remembering those "drop and roll" drills from your school days; this is a handy skill to have when you're the parent of a toddler. Just switch it to "drop and sleep." After all, the kitchen floor can be a very comfortable place to grab a quick, one-minute nap, particularly if you roll toward the refrigerator, where the motor has made the floor warm.

Get used to the one-minute nap. There is hardly anything a toddler resents more than the idea that all conscious brain activity is going to have to cease for a while. They see themselves as well on their way to ownership of the entire world, and sleep is a miserable interruption of their conquests, and they want as little of it as possible.

The trouble is, the rest of the world feels that you are the one in control of the situation. You are supposed to be able to make your child go to sleep.

Is that a hilarious notion, or what? Toddlers know lots more about not falling asleep than you know about getting them to go to sleep, and frankly, they're a lot less tired than you are and have a lot more free time. Plus, they have a secret weapon: They know that you know that they can now stand up and climb and knock over huge pieces of furniture and leap out of windows and otherwise kill themselves in a million different ways, and somehow they divine that it is your job to prevent this from happening. They are fairly confident, when you are letting them "cry it out" in their rooms, that they can get you right back in there anytime they want.

Not that they're sophisticated enough to yell, "I'm quite capable of inflicting damage, you know!" Instead, you'll be downstairs, and you'll hear the unmistakable sound of the closet door being ripped from its hinges, smashed into the window, and then the changing table being hurled out into the backyard, followed soon after by the crib and the rocking chair.

Well, what are you going to do? Stand there and mutter to yourself about how the books say don't go in there for any reason whatsoever, or are you going to dash upstairs, praying that you get there before the baby himself sails through the window on his crib bumpers? Obviously you have to run.

Any number of hideous things await you. Once, my friend Elise threw open the bedroom door to find her now-diaperless baby standing on the rocking chair, busily coating the wallpaper with the ample contents of her former diaper. Her child—who had never before managed to venture outside the crib—had ingeniously stacked up all the stuffed animals to boost herself out of her prison.

But that's nothing. Once I went tearing upstairs, after innumerable crashing noises, to find that I couldn't open the door at all. My sixteen-month-old had gotten out of the crib, and somehow managed to push the dresser over to the door. God knows what had motivated this fit of redecorating, but now he was screaming piteously, having realized too late that he was trapped in the room.

"Next time," I told him through the keyhole, "remember that the larger furniture pieces really do belong against the walls."

This is the trouble with toddlers: They have grown out of their reptilian brain stage and now have essentially the brains of chimpanzees. Sure, they're well on their way to being human beings, but you wouldn't want to place any bets on whether they're actually going to get there.

Still, you'd like to improve their odds if you can, which means following them around, never even taking your eyes off them, until you are reasonably sure that they have fallen sound asleep-,which is such a medical rarity as to be worthy of being written up in the journals. Once, our toddler fell asleep on the carpet in the living room, and I got so excited seeing a child legally sleeping that I phoned my husband at work to describe the sight of him. Naturally the sound of the buttons being pressed on the phone woke the kid right up, and he was off again.

The nights are not much better. Once they are able to escape the confines of their cages, nothing is safe anymore. Those middle-of-the-night noises you usually dismiss as just being the cats playing toothpaste-cap hockey on the bathroom floor? Not anymore they aren't. Chances are The Kid is making a comeback in some other room in your house, and you would do well to get yourself down there and put a stop to the party before it gets out of hand—or worse, moves outdoors into traffic. I went downstairs once at 3:25 A.M. to find all the lights on, the stereo and television set blaring, and my naked two-year-old jumping on the living room couch cushions, wearing only my rain hat.

As I lugged him upstairs, reloaded him into his diaper and pajamas, and tucked him back into my bed, where I could keep a reasonably half-focused eye on him for the rest of the night, it occurred to me that he could have been doing anything: turning on the stove, climbing into the refrigerator, heading out the front door. I began to wonder if maybe putting chicken wire over the top of the crib would be too cruel an option—and how it would fit into our decorating scheme, which up until then had been yellow ducks and blue bunnies. We'd foolishly rejected the prison scheme when we were thinking up how we wanted the baby's room to look, but now bars on the window and manacles in the crib were beginning to sound like just the thing.

105

There is a trick to getting kids to sleep— no one knows what it is, though

Some people believe they know how to get children to go to sleep. There are even some parents who think they've got the secret, and these are the most infuriating of all people. It is good not to have too much to do with these kinds of people, because they will quickly convince you that you are inferior, when you are perfectly normal and sane. Once, at a party, I almost smacked a father who was going on and on about how he and his wife had utter control of their child's sleep schedule.

"If we want her to sleep, we just put her in the crib, say goodnight, and off she goes without a whimper," he boasted. "And the best part is, we decide when that will be. If we need her out of the way, we sometimes put her to bed at six at night. Other nights, it might be eight-thirty or even ten."

I couldn't believe my ears. Here he was, talking to a roomful of bleary-eyed, sleep-deprived parents—and he was shamelessly bragging about this mutant child he'd somehow managed to produce. Some people at the party fawned over the man and his wife, oohing and ahhing and then asking for advice. By this time, the guy was leaning against the fireplace, looking like Clark Gable, as he said, "You just have to be firm. The baby has to know, deep down, that you mean every word of it. It's bedtime, and that's just the way it is." He jabbed the air with his index finger. "It's really the first rule of parenthood: You make the rules."

Three years later, I ran into him at the park one day. We were both wearily chasing unruly toddlers and fruitlessly attempting to keep everybody from eating handfuls of sand in the sandbox. He looked more tired than anybody I'd seen since looking in the mirror that morning. I mean, his blinks were at least thirty seconds each, and at one point I would swear that he snored between words in a sentence.

He and his wife had had another child, and this one was normal. Oh, sure, the other one could still fall asleep on command, but this new one was showing them a thing or two.

He said mournfully, "The worst part is, I really thought we knew what we were doing."

I tried to be kind. I really wanted to be nice about it. I leaned over and patted his arm and told him that, really, it wasn't his fault.

"But," I said, "I really do think you need to get the telephone numbers of all those parents who listened to you three years ago and call them all up. You do owe everyone an apology, you know."

Since then, I've learned not to listen to anyone who has the slightest bit of condescending advice on getting small children to go to sleep. I've had to conclude that some kids like sleep, and most of them don't and that even the ones who like going to sleep will go through long stretches when they wake up every few minutes through the night because they're teething, or they have a cold, or just because they decided it would be nice to see you again.

By the time our third non-sleeping child had come along, we had decided to make some ironclad rules about what could and could not take place in the middle of the night. We were very ferocious about these being enforced.

Rules for Toddlers in the Middle of the Night

- No cookies. Snacks are to be limited to those that come from the mother's body.
- Self-removal of diaper or other clothing is prohibited.
- No climbing out of the crib and chasing the cats with the toy lawn mower.
- Do not even think of suggesting a trip downstairs to watch *Barney* videos, listen to the *Sesame Street* tape, or reenact yesterday's after-bath towel dance.

- No sharp objects or electrical appliances will be procured for you past midnight. Anything other than a teddy bear that you neglected to bring to bed will have to stay in its proper place until morning.
- No getting up before 5:00 A.M. simply because you think you can eat the dog treats before the dog wakes up.

You have each other to sleep with, so let the kid have the toaster

Along about the first birthday, it occurs to the kid that you have an incredible advantage over her when it comes to falling asleep: You have your own person in the bed with you. She also wants a husband. In fact, she demands that a husband be procured for her immediately. She doesn't know that husbands steal the covers, put their cold feet on you during the night, and think up adventurous playtime activities when you're too tired to even draw consecutive breaths. To her, it looks like nothing but fun.

And let's face it: Despite all of the disadvantages, it is fun. You mostly would not wish your husband to be sleeping elsewhere, even though he snores, has cold feet, and can remember that you once liked making love all night long.

Since obviously you can't very well find the baby a mate—there just aren't that many other babies available for marriage in this country—and you certainly don't want to install her in your bed for the rest of time, there will be lots of complicated negotiations that will take place. Time after time, baby after baby, I found myself somehow negotiated into a deal where I agreed to stay with the reluctant sleeper until she had fallen into stage-four sleep.

I hated this. For one thing, unlike the kid, who could go on for hours, I was usually out cold within a few minutes of lying down. And it would sometimes be past midnight before I managed to stir myself out of the bed and make my way back downstairs and remember that I had an adult life. By that time, I'd be cranky and stiff and resentful—and so well rested on my few hours of sleep that I'd spend the middle-of-the-night hours staring at the ceiling, listening to the house settle, and wondering why I majored in English literature and if I'd have enough money to pay the taxes ten years from now.

This was when I discovered the Bedtime Buddy System.

I warn you, it takes a certain amount of flexibility to embrace this system, which means that instead of letting your baby get married right away or deciding that you are the lifetime bedmate, you have to let him sleep with something else.

I know what you're thinking. You're thinking teddy bear. Maybe a stuffed doggie, or one of those fluffy little bunny rabbits who wear vests.

This is not what the child is likely to think of.

My friend Suzanne had a kid who insisted on sleeping with the family's toaster, all because he'd seen an animated toaster on a cartoon show and so was convinced that the toaster was lonely in the kitchen at night all by itself. So Suzanne found herself reluctantly tucking the toaster in every night (wrapping the cord around itself twenty times), and then in the morning, she would have to retrieve it from the bedroom so she could make breakfast.

Worse was my son, who demanded to be bedded down each night with the set of screwdrivers, an avocado pit, and my grandmother's antique Chinese napkin rings.

You may argue for a while about these things, but there will come a time when you realize that you're actually relieved to see the screwdrivers find a nice comfortable bed for themselves, especially if it means you get to have your own bed. You are thrilled, in fact, to see how this is all working out.

I was telling my husband about this ingenious solution, when the look on his face stopped me cold.

"What?" I said. "Surely you can do without the screwdrivers for the night, can't you?"

"Do you hear what you're saying?" he said. "You're actually going to put our toddler to bed with five sharp objects?"

I went back to renegotiate the bedtime deal.

You might as well know, going into this, that a kid who has determined that screwdrivers need to accompany him off to dreamland probably isn't going to be flexible about leaving them in the garage. I had to rehearse my strategy all day long before I went back to the deal-making table.

"Darling," I said, "the screwdrivers need pajamas before they can go to sleep. They have to sleep in this little leather pouch."

Fortunately, the idea of screwdrivers in pajamas was even more attractive than naked screwdrivers, so I was able to win that one without much trouble. Nature doesn't often smile on you so benevolently, you know.

But then, once I was in bed, I realized there were other worries. What if the kid woke up in the middle of the night and decided to do some home repair projects? What if, say, the electrical outlet suddenly seemed as though it needed to be dismantled? Or the bars of the crib removed?

I lay awake for hours, imagining all the worst possible things.

Every now and then I'd whisper to my husband, "Did you ever tell him not to put objects in the electrical outlets? Did you? Well, did you?"

At last he got up on one elbow and stared at me. "The kid is sixteen months old. We haven't covered electricity yet."

This is where parenthood gets its bad reputation, and it's best if you don't talk about this aspect to other, childless, people. I had to spend the next week doing a whole explanation on how screwdrivers are very, very grouchy if they don't get a full night's sleep, and that one must never think of taking them out of their leather pajamas or otherwise disturbing them when everybody else in the house is sleeping.

"The screwdrivers," I said, "really need to be with Daddy or Mommy before you take them out of their leather pajamas."

"Avocado seed need pajamas too," said the kid.

So that's how I came to spend an otherwise nice afternoon stitching up a pair of flowered pajamas for our family's avocado seed. Later, I figured, I could maybe shop for something becoming for the antique Chinese napkin rings.

Sneaky Sleep

It's tough to believe, but toddlers manage to figure out a kind of sleep that you hate for them to get. This is just the beginning of their careers as Loophole Finders—it's long and steady work through the years of childhood.

Yes, you pray for them to sleep.

No, you don't want Sneaky Sleep.

Naturally, this is the kind of slumber they adore the most. It's the kind that takes place at such random intervals that it hardly seems to count. The car—your former sleep aid from the baby days—has now become the enemy. Strap a toddler in the car seat—even for a five-minute trip to the Stop & Shop for milk and bread—and blam! He's out like a light before you get to the end of your driveway.

And then, when you get to the Stop & Shop, you'll have to lug this child (who has now expanded his weight tenfold by some mysterious process that only happens in connection with sleep) through the vegetable aisle, down through the dairy and meats and over past the breads. By the time you get to the checkout counter, somehow shoving the cart along with your elbows and knees, you will be walking in a permanently stooped-over position, and your child will be in sleep so deep people are inquiring about a pulse.

This is Sneaky Sleep. For reasons we can't know, this fifteen-minute nap will cancel out any need for sleep for the rest of the day, and may even contaminate the next day and, in some cases, mess up the following week as well. In fact, my friend Ellie traces her adolescent daughter's need to stay up all night to a ten-minute nap she took once on the way to the dry cleaners back when she was nineteen months old.

You have to prevent Sneaky Sleep at all costs. This will take quite a bit of energy, but after one or two midnights spent trying to think up entertainment for an insomniac toddler, you will sadly realize all the things you could have done to keep this sleep problem from happening in the first place.

What might you have done?

My favorite is shouting. I spent whole years when, if I were riding in the car with my toddler, I would keep up a high-volume patter of small child humor. I did jokes, anecdotes, *Sesame Street* impressions. (I learned, for instance, to imitate Bert saying, "Hot chili pepper," and I suggest this might be a good thing to start practicing in the shower. It's a skill you'll have all your life.) I pointed out signs and read them aloud. I discoursed on the preponderance of blue cars. I talked about bugs and Grandma—and then even the bugs that might be on Grandma.

And when all this seemed to be failing, and I could see through the rearview mirror that the kid's eyes were falling to half mast, I was not too proud to start chanting: "No sleep! No sleep! No sleep!"

This, at least, was good for a laugh from the kid. They find it uproariously funny that you've spent about a million hours urging, pleading, and threatening them into sleep—and that now you've come around to the other side and have even invented a chant to keep them from falling asleep.

Forget the jokes about Grandma's bugs. To a toddler's sensibilities, this is the stuff of raw comedy: an adult acting out of character. Folks, it doesn't get any better than that.

Chapter 8: The Daddy Dance

It's a long road from husband to daddy

There's not much these days that a man can get out of simply because he has a penis.

It used to be that a penis could buy a person a lot of downtime. People who had them got to go away to a mysterious "office" every day and then come home and demand rest afterwards, on the theory that this "office" had gotten them so worn out and grouchy that they could not possibly be expected to help with such things as dinner preparations, small children, and dog shit on the rug.

But then women went to work. That's when offices were exposed for what they really are: places where people mostly stand around and drink coffee, take things called breaks, and then indulge in a flurry of phone calls—some of them non-personal—before they tackle fifteen minutes of work-related activities and get ready to go home.

Men, it was decided, had better start mustering the energy to help raise the kids.

And then, through perfect reasonableness, it was decided that if men were going to be there for the raising, then it naturally followed that they had to be there to appreciate when the babies came out. They were to stand in the delivery room and say things like, "Push! Breathe!" and, when it seemed appropriate, "It's okay! I promise this won't happen again!"

They had to be there, not only so they could appreciate how much physical trauma was involved and see for themselves the correct spot for cutting an umbilical cord, but also so they could do that instantaneous bonding with babies that would keep them from minding too much when the baby screamed all night long for three weeks.

Mostly this has worked out great for everybody. Guys, now getting in on the ground floor, feel sorrier for their wives than they used to, and they're willing to change more diapers. Women have someone to scream at in the delivery room besides the labor nurses. And doctors no longer have to shoulder the responsibility of snipping the umbilical cord all by themselves.

"When is this kid going to DO something?"

There's one little drawback about guys getting in right on the ground floor. They tend to be a little impatient with the normal course of things. It used to be that the first real one-on-one involvement for many dads was teaching the kid to ride a two-wheeler on a Saturday afternoon, or, in some cases, sharing a six-pack sometime after college. If you're looking for an action- packed, me-and-you-as-pals kind of relationship, then the Brand New Baby act is going to seem a little boring.

Men tend to stand over the bassinet, twitching, waiting for something fun to take place.

"But look at all he can do now!" his wife says. "He can hiccup, sneeze, wave his little arms in the air—it's just amazing. Yesterday I noticed he mostly waved his right arm, so I wrote down in the baby book that he's probably right-handed, but today he's giving equal time to the left, so I just don't know. Let's sit here together and watch him to see what the rest of the day brings."

This is not enough to hold most men's attention. You can entertain a man with infant bodily function reports only so much—about one burp and maybe a sneeze per day—but if anything else takes place, like if the baby smacks his lips in his sleep, you'd better have somebody else you can call about it, or you'll go crazy.

My friend Maggie, upon hearing it was me on the phone for the fifth time one day, said, "Oh, hi. Don't tell me there was another Lip Smacking Sighting."

"Not so much that this time. I think I saw an actual tongue thrust, and then he made kind of an oohing sound in his sleep."

Maggie said, "I hope you're writing all this down," and I do not think she was being sarcastic. She knew.

I don't know why it is that most men don't go in for this kind of thing. Sure, it has its slow moments, but you want to tell me that Major League Baseball is a riveting experience all the time? You have to explain to them that it's the waiting for something to happen that's part of the fun. It's the tension, see. You sit there watching a sleeping baby, butt thrust up in the air, arms curled up tight next to the chin—and then, when the silence becomes excruciating, there'll be a burp. It's great.

But as if burping, peeing, spitting up, and tongue-thrusting aren't already full-time enterprises, oftentimes dads want proof that this baby is indeed a Sterling Specimen of Personhood. You'll see him in the baby's room, counting and recounting the toes and fingers, examining the birthmarks under a magnifying glass, and running subtle little tests. ("Margaret? How do we know these fingernails and toenails are really going to grow? Could you ask the pediatrician if these are normal on the next visit?")

I know one new father who used to like to hurl himself into the baby's line of vision, just to see the baby startle. It turned out that he was not trying to raise a neurotic child, as some people thought; it was just that he needed constant assurances that the baby could, indeed, see and hear. His friends all thought this was a bit extreme of him when,

116

after all, there wasn't any evidence of blindness or deafness, but this guy kept insisting that you never could tell about these things and you had to keep a constant vigil until the kid could tell you herself. Later, his friends were able to get him a job, beta-testing computer programs— and his child does seem to be normal, except that she leaps in the air whenever anyone comes near her.

Things Dads Can Do While Waiting for the Baby to Get Interesting

- Practice blowing on bellies.
- Learn all the words to "The Wheels on the Bus," including engine parts.
- Develop an impressive car noise for those nights when the baby can't sleep and you don't want to ride around in the real car.
- Tighten up the floorboards in the baby's room so you can make an escape without the baby waking up.
- Perfect a comic riff that makes the baby laugh— saying nonsense words like "boozha boozha" works great, as do impressions of Pluto and Mickey Mouse. (Groucho Marx will do in a pinch.)
- Figure out how to rewind the baby swing without it screeching.

In defense of the changing table

It must be said that there are some other minor differences between mothers and fathers, and most of them have to do with furniture.

I have yet to meet a man who realizes in advance that his house is going to need a changing table. For some reason, this is the item—this innocent little place where a baby can get her diapers changed in peace—that makes men feel that their whole lives are being swamped and overrun by parenthood. A man hearing for the first time that his wife wants to buy a changing table is like a man hearing that the two of them will never again be able to take a vacation alone.

He has a whole list of reasons why a changing table is the most extravagant, ridiculous purchase in the whole world, but none of them makes much sense to a pregnant woman who's already able to picture what it's going to be like to change the new baby's diapers. Here's the list of things I've heard:

- They're just temporary pieces of furniture, so it's stupid to buy one.
- You can't do anything with them afterwards.
- They take up space.
- You can change the baby on (pick one) the floor, the bed, the kitchen counter, the hood of the car.
- We'll just have to move it again when we move out of this house twenty years from now.
- You let one changing table in and pretty soon you've got a whole furniture outlet thing going here.
- We've got to start saving money for braces and college so we can't be squandering it on crap.

Women find this resistance to pieces of furniture very strange, of course. It's like taking exception to the necessity for tables and chairs. In fact, we try to figure it out when we get together in private.

"He understood about the crib, the car seat, the stroller, the windup swing, the diaper bag, and even the plastic bathtub," my friend Ellie told a group of women at the playground one day. "But he said it would be a huge mistake to buy a changing table."

"How can it be a huge mistake to change the baby's diapers? I think, in fact, it's illegal not to change the diapers," someone told her.

"We can change the diapers. We just have to do it on the floor."

Beth's husband reluctantly agreed to a changing table, but drew the line at a plastic bathtub. He was sure getting one of those blue plastic tubs was the beginning of a Baby Items Infiltration Project that would begin and would take over his life and free time, and possibly have some untoward result on his sexual performance as well.

"A little harmless molded plastic bathtub, with a nice sloping area to lay the baby on while you wash him," said Beth. "Where's the harm? I told him we could turn it into a planter once the baby had outgrown it."

Frankly, I don't think these fights are about the objects at all. I think it's the way the reality of parenthood sneaks up on us. One day it's the pink line on the pregnancy test, and the next thing you know you're no longer young and virile, besides which the college tuition bills are due.

In between, though, you really do need a changing table—or your back will hurt from changing diapers on the floor.

Everybody loves a guy with a baby

There's something a little weird about the world that I feel I must warn you of. It's a little schizoid on the subject of parents and children. For instance, let a man walk down the street with a baby slung over his shoulder, and everyone who sees him will stop and sigh wistfully after him. But let a woman take to the streets with her baby, and if anyone even notices her in the first place, what they're thinking is, *Hmmm. Is she just letting her professional life go, now that she's a mother? And can't she comb her hair?*

No one knows for sure why this is. I suspect it has something to do with the advertising industry, which years ago happened upon the discovery that big macho men looked sort of cute diapering babies, and that women would go out and buy disposable diapers if someone like, say, Arnold Schwarzenegger or James Earl Jones was applying them to a baby's bottom. Or maybe it's just another one of those millennium kind of things that we won't understand until anthropologists explain it to us hundreds of years from now. But whatever its cause, men with babies get star treatment, and women with babies don't. A woman carrying a baby in a Snugli is likely to hear from strangers that she's probably damaging the child's neck, carrying it that way, or that she's raising a future psychopath because he wasn't allowed to face forward while in transit. Once an elderly woman risked her life to cross a busy street to rush over to explain to me that I was most likely crushing my baby's very pliable nose, having him plastered onto my chest that way.

After I explained that these things are designed with the nose health of the babies well in mind, she stared at me for a long moment.

"You new mothers are so selfish," she said. "Did you ever stop to think whether or not it's even interesting for a baby to stare at your chest like that for hours and hours?"

I tried to draw myself up with some dignity, even though I was feeling a little wobbly from this attack. "Actually, my chest happens to be one of his favorite sites in the whole world," I told her.

I guess I don't have to tell you that this would not happen to a guy. Let a father strap on a baby, and instantly there are people lined up to praise him for his involvement with his kid and to suggest that perhaps he is tired and couldn't they please assist him by changing the child's poopy diaper while he relaxes with a beer. I have seen this happen with my own eyes. And, oh, just let a man make some horrible parenting mistake in public, and women are all around him to reassure him that he's perfectly normal, nothing to worry about. I think that if, by some stunning degree of ignorance or mismanagement on his part, a new father were even to strap the baby in the Snugli upside down, with the baby's little legs kicking him in the chin, people would simply chuckle at such adorability in one large human.

120

Not to belabor the point, but I have even seen men show up at work—at work!—with their babies, only to have the entire secretarial staff voluntarily shut down their operations so they could spirit the baby away for the rest of the day while the dad got his work done.

"Oh, the poor thing!" they coo—and I do not think they mean the baby. I think that for complicated biological and deep-seated guilty reasons, women start feeling so sorry for a guy who's in charge of a baby that they will do anything to protect him from having to take care of the baby and work at the same time. Maybe it's just that they know from experience that such a combination doesn't ever work out and they don't want men to suspect how difficult life really is. I don't know. This is a primitive area here, and I can't hope to trace the origins of these feelings. All I know is that a guy with a kid is thought to be a major superhero, worthy of citations and awards.

But just let a woman bring the baby in for fifteen minutes while she picks up her work stuff on a day when the caregiver didn't show up—and there is no end of the people who will point out that she's certainly not very serious about her job, lugging that kid around like she does.

"So unprofessional," they'll say. "And look at that spit-up on the shoulder of her dress."

Guys are thought to look darling with spit-up on the shoulders of their nicest blue suits. And if they really want to gather up some oohs and ahhs, they should never leave home without a pacifier sticking out of their breast pocket. (For God's sake, make sure it's a spare. You don't want to be responsible for leaving home with the only working pacifier.) And for maximum effect, you can't beat a newborn-sized Huggies falling out of the briefcase every now and then. (No extra points for it being a dirty one, however.)

For men: Things it's good to say to your wife

I'm sure I don't have to point out that your wife has been through a lot. Getting to be the person in the couple who actually reproduces the species is terrific and all that, but there's something slightly horrifying about the moment when you stand up for the first time after giving birth and that mantle of skin that so politely stretched out so it could contain the baby for the whole nine months—well, it sort of collapses. There's no other word for it. It just hangs there, like an old apron or something. If you are the woman this is happening to, your first thought is probably not going to be how great it is to have this divine little baby in your life from now on. It runs along the lines of: *Oh, my God! What have I done to myself?*

This is where dads come in. You cannot be the one to notice all that extra skin. Pretend with all your might that it isn't there. Because it won't be there in another couple of weeks. Believe me, if it didn't go away, most women would be hitting their stomach skin with their knees when they walked down the street, and we hardly ever see that happening.

There are, I'm afraid, lots of things you can't say in the first few months. For instance, I think it's considered grounds for divorce if you say what my friend George said to his wife when she was worried about losing the last ten pounds of weight she'd gained in pregnancy. He said, "Well, if you'd cut back at the old feedbag, I think you'd lose it in no time." Later he said he meant it in the kindest, jokiest way possible.

It's possible that it's too late for poor George to repair the damage he did to his relationship with his wife, but surely all the rest of us can agree that the word feedbag has no place between a man and his wife, unless they work on a farm together.

Also, while we're on the subject, there has to be a moratorium on discussions involving your observations of other women's slimness. If she should bring up somebody else's stunning figure, remember that this could be a trap. It's best to think up a reason to drop to the floor and forget to notice. Maybe there's some rewiring project you need to get to suddenly, to keep the house from possibly blowing up.

Ordering bathing suits or lacy teddies for "later" is not a good idea either. She is also not interested in how quickly the women at your office—or your mother—bounced back from childbirth, as compared to her own more gradual progress.

Still, there are things it's important to say to her that will be appreciated, now and forever:

- "You make motherhood look so beautiful. I think it's so cool how your breasts now know how to squirt milk when we're making love."
- "Yes, you do look like you've lost all your baby weight."
- "I think being able to get dressed in the morning is really overrated anyhow."
- "Those aren't bags under your eyes. That's just part of your glow now that you are a mom."
- "From now on, I want to be the one who gets up with the baby in the middle of the night so you can get your rest."
- "So we'll eat out for the next few months, if you're tired. I'll bring home takeout tonight."
- "Sex is so beside the point. Can't we just cuddle?"
- "God, I'm glad we got that changing table."

Chapter 9: Milkies and Ninnies

Getting in touch with your bovine side

There is nothing like breast-feeding to make you feel talented. Your body, which until labor at least has not shown you much in the way of impressive physical feats, has now turned out to be brilliant in its ability to produce milk. Milk—an actually useful substance! And your body makes it in its own little factory, without instructions or even effort from you. All the baby has to do is whimper a bit, and presto! Your breasts automatically let loose a stream of rich, creamy, body-temperature, designed-just-for-her milk.

So what that most of it lands on the front of you—or, in extreme cases, on the wall across the room? Sometimes there's not a baby's mouth around precisely when you need it.

But that's okay. You get used to the fact that your entire torso is going to be mostly wet for the first few weeks, and that stray kittens are going to be circling your house, waiting for a chance to run inside and leap onto your chest. This is the new you—indispensable to an infant and adored by cats.

When you're nursing, you also forget that most people don't consider breasts a working part of people's anatomy. You get so comfortable with the idea of them that you forget that in our culture they're basically sex objects, considered useful mainly for their ability to sell cars and beer on television. After just a few short weeks of knowing them in this new way, as food sources, you may get to the point where you haul them out just anywhere, the same as you'd do with your elbow, for instance, if it could come up with a useful purpose for itself.

In fact, I once answered the front door without remembering to fully button up my shirt, and could not figure out for the longest time why the UPS guy stood there, staring at me in disbelief, and then could barely get the words out to ask me to sign the receipt. I went back in the house, shaking my head, thinking how strange a creature he was.

UPS drivers' reactions notwithstanding, there are some very wonderful reasons for breast-feeding a baby, not the least of which is that you get to have more minutes of sleep than other new parents, simply because you don't have to schlep downstairs in the middle of the night to fix a bottle. Some people, though, will tell you all sorts of bad things about nursing: that it will ultimately ruin your figure, make you smell like a dairy most of the time, and keep your husband from taking his rightful turn feeding the baby.

I say anything beats standing in front of a microwave in the middle of the night, waiting for a bottle of formula to get to the precisely correct temperature. And as for fathers not getting to feed the baby, so? He can do other things: change the diapers, for instance.

The day the milk comes in—and other screamingly happy events

Your breasts don't simply begin making milk right there on the delivery table, you know. Maybe it's that the news of the baby's birth travels northward very slowly, or maybe breasts are really philosophical entities that need some time to think things over. I think they carefully consider the matter before they give the order to start the milk-making process. It's not easy getting all the pumps primed and cleaning out the ducts. They don't want to go to all that trouble if later it's going to turn out they didn't have to.

In the meantime, just to keep the baby from starving to death, they put out a thin, clear liquid called colostrum, the function of which seems to be to make your never-having-breast-fed elderly relatives declare that you'll never be able to nourish a human being on that watery stuff.

But then, along about Day Three, the milk factory opens with great fanfare and enthusiasm. Usually your breasts actually wake you up from a sound sleep with their announcement: "THE MILK IS HERE! DID SOMEBODY ORDER SOME MILK? WHERE'S THE BABY? WE'VE GOT ENOUGH MILK FOR THIS BABY AND ANY OTHER BABIES IN THE NEIGHBORHOOD AS WELL! EVERYBODY UP!"

If you're sleeping on your stomach, you will find that your breasts are so huge that chances are your torso and feet are not even touching the bed. You look like somebody strapped two bed pillows to the front of you. It'd be great to stop to pose for some photos to send to your old friends from seventh grade except that you find you are in a massive hurry to find the baby's mouth.

Naturally this is probably the day your baby has decided to catch up on all that sleep he's been lacking since birth, and so you'll find yourself prying open his jaws and begging him to remember how to suck.

"Remember all that thin, watery stuff you've had to put up with over the last few days?" you say. "It's not like that anymore. We've got the real thing for you now. It's worth waking up for."

Sometimes a baby will indicate he would prefer to sleep now and eat later, thank you very much. This kind of baby, you can be assured, is also going to be the kind of teenager who will someday drive you crazy by sleeping until noon. However, when he's a teenager, you'll be able to jump up and down, call his name, open his shades, and insist that he get the hell up. Right now, I'm afraid there's not much you can do to reason with him.

My friend Sally once carefully explained to her sleeping three-day-old son that he was going to be grounded just as soon as he was old enough to want to leave the house, unless he got himself organized and drank up some of that milk she'd made for him.

I think it was at that point that the baby actually started snoring.

Sally then said, "All right, fine. Then I'm going to go out and find some other hungry, cooperative babies who will appreciate the wonderful milk I've made for them, and then when you want some later, you're just going to find yourself out of luck."

He did one of those fleeting little sleep smiles, obviously mocking her.

"And just wait until two in the morning when you want to get up and nurse! See who's sorry then!"

It was at that moment that Sally realized it had taken her only three days to start sounding exactly like her mother.

Pumping milk

This brings us to the breast pump.

The breast pump, you see, lets you fill up little plastic baggies with milk, which is handy when the baby couldn't care less that you, his long-suffering mother, are filled to the brim with heavy, warm milk that you want out of your body now. It is also handy for those times that you and your breasts aren't going to be immediately available to the baby, and that other people, whose breasts aren't so talented as yours, are going to need to have something to give the kid.

The thing is, you have to get the milk to go into those little baggies. It's quite a shock to discover that milk, which seems to flow so bountifully even when you wish it wouldn't, refuses to leap into those bags, courtesy of your wishes alone. It has to be coaxed there, since your breasts are quite aware that there is no baby suckling at them. Breasts can be pretty stubborn about knowing that their mission is to feed babies, and not simply to fill up bags for the population at large. I mean, they're willing to show off a little, but they resent people taking advantage of them. Therefore, they have got to be tricked.

Luckily, this being a time in history when no desire for trickery goes unmet for very long by folks who know how to market things, we have pumps. I know what you're thinking. And yes, it is almost a cow thing, but that's what motherhood does for you. You'll find that you're getting in touch with that part of yourself that has a lot in common with cows. You will really start to admire how cows conduct their daily lives, as a matter of fact.

My first pump was a rubber bulb attached to a glass tube that fit over my nipple as long as I held it in place. With this kind of contraption, if you squeeze the bulb thousands of times, perhaps while meditating about flowing rivers and simultaneously listening to a tape of infants crying, it is possible to extract, say, about one ounce for every twenty-four hours of constant, uninterrupted usage. I used to sit and watch the milk drip down, one hard-won drop at a time, and wish that I could just wring out my nursing bra into the plastic bag instead.

Then someone told me that to get the best milk production (and I have to tell you that the word production spoken in relation to your own dear body parts is quite a shock at first), a person could pump one breast while actually nursing the baby on the other breast. But this turned out to require a staff of at least three people—one to keep the baby from falling on the floor, one to hold the pump and do the squeezing, and one to keep the plastic bag in place.

128

I don't have to tell you that in this day and age, it's tough to find that kind of help. Also—and this is what you don't realize going into this—breast pumping has a way of making you feel truly mammalian, in a way that nursing a baby does not. Babies are soft and round and warm and make sweet little guzzling noises. Breast pumps can't help but make you think of barnyards. You may not want anyone there to watch you.

This is when you might want to invest in an electric pump.

Trying not to think about Bessie the faithful cow, you hook yourself up—two breasts, no waiting—flip the switch with your toes, and whoosh! Your breasts are emptied out in a matter of minutes. You don't have to think about babies' gums nuzzling against you or the flowing rivers of the world to get your breasts in the mood. They have no choice but to give up all that they have created. In fact, you feel somewhat lucky that your internal organs were spared being vacuumed up and whisked right out of your body. That would be quite a thing to find in the little plastic baggie, wouldn't it? Your spleen, floating there in the milk.

Oh, well. It's best not to think of these things. As far as I know, no woman's spleen has ever been sucked out by the breast pump. And the good thing about using the electric breast pump—poetically called the Blue Lactina, I believe—is that the whole pump-and-go process is over very fast. Long before anyone can come in and catch you doing it.

But if your husband should come in and discover you, try not to freak him out by mooing at him.

Nursing in public—without taking all your clothes off

I always thought that an exhibitionist could have a great career as a breast-feeding mother. She could simply strip down completely and sit there, basking in her motherhood while being stared at by the world at the same time.

Most of us, however, are constantly trying to figure out ways of keeping ourselves reasonably decent so that customers in restaurants won't come over and start screeching at us for ruining their appetites by feeding our babies. This means that, for a while at least, you have to give up the darling black dress that zips up the back, unless you want to carry with you a double bed-sized blanket to wrap yourself up in while you've hiked up the dress for nursing.

The good news is that almost anything you can pull up is terrific for breast-feeding. You'd think that a shirt you could unbutton would be best, but in fact, it's better to yank it up than unfasten it, because less of your actual flesh gets flashed to the public at large. You are also allowed to drape yourself with blankets and cloth diapers and paper towels and anything else that makes you feel like a well-dressed, inconspicuous breast-feeder.

My friend Jeanne, who took modesty to rather an extreme, resembled a mummy whenever she was nursing. You could tell her baby was hungry when Jeanne methodically started unpacking tablecloths, bed sheets, and blankets out of the suitcase she laughingly called a diaper bag. By the time she had wrapped herself and the baby up, there wasn't so much as one millimeter of flesh showing, and once I was tempted to offer her a snorkel just to make sure she could breathe in there.

She may not have had nipples waving at the world at large, but people stared at her just the same.

Nursing bras—which are so attractive that they look as though the government, the army, and the CIA all got together and designed them— have clasps that allow you to get to the useful part of your breast without having to do too much shimmying around and unhooking stuff. Some of them even have pouches where you can insert little pads (they look like half-size sanitary napkins) to soak up some of the leaks that are bound to happen. By the time you get all dressed up in your industrial-strength bra, with the nursing pads shoved in, you look like you're so top- heavy you're in danger of landing on your face. Don't be surprised if teenage boys honk their horns at you on the street.

Still, the first few times you nurse in public can be unnerving. I remember once breast-feeding my four-month-old son in the bank, being absolutely frantic to keep all our offensive parts buried under various cloth diapers so that absolutely no one would guess that something as gross as a meal was taking place. He had been sucking madly for a few minutes, so the milk flow was well under way, when somebody across the room sneezed.

Many babies could probably let a sneeze take place without having to halt their lunch, leap in the air, and swivel their heads around, but not mine. He was deeply fascinated by other people's noises—and it was just a shame in his view that breasts weren't detachable so he could move around at will while he nursed.

Naturally, breasts aren't equipped with a good set of brakes, so the milk continued to spurt all over the place, much to my horror, including onto the dapper gentleman seated next to us. I sat, frozen in place, as he stared at the drops on his arm. He held out his arm to gaze at it from a distance, then he pulled it right up to his eyeballs. He sniffed it and jiggled it.

I prayed that three drops of milk would not have a dairy-type smell. I prayed that he wouldn't notice how white the glistening drops were. Let's face it: I prayed for a trapdoor to open up and plunge my baby and me into the bank's basement.

Then the old gentleman looked up and examined the ceiling very carefully. Later, I heard him telling the guard that he hoped the bank's money was safe from the leaky roof.

131

The perfect weaning moment: What if you were on the phone when it came?

Nursing will hardly be under way when some kind souls will inquire when you're going to stop. They will say this in the tone of voice they would use if you had taken up something like voodoo, or if you had announced your intention to stitch your fingers and toes together in your spare time.

They will be concerned.

"Don't go on too long," they'll say, trying to sound jocular about it, "or else the college dean won't let him get his degree, you know."

We both know why they say these things. They're terrified that now that you're hanging out your bazoombas whenever you feel like it, maybe you won't ever stop. People get a little mixed up between feeding babies and exhibitionism. You can try to educate them and they'll pretend to be listening, but actually what they're hoping for is that you'll say, "Oh, all right. Nursing is a filthy, disgusting habit, and I've decided to give it up before I get so excited I start looking for work as a stripper."

In spite of the fact that Haveyoustoppednursingyet will be the first question on anyone's lips whenever they call you up, the surgeon general of the United States, no less, has said we're allowed to nurse our babies as long as we want to. He may not have heard the rumors about the college deans, though.

A good thing to remind yourself is that hardly any college-age kids are interested in nursing, especially from their moms. There will come a point when a baby looks around and realizes that other people aren't getting fed in the same style she is, and she decides she'd rather be like everyone else. (Call it early peer pressure if you want to.) Or else she gets bothered by the fact that breasts do seem to be stubbornly attached to the front of the mom, making it difficult to see all the goings-on while nursing.

For some babies, these two flaws are enough to make them decide that nursing just isn't worth it—and there will come a time when you offer the breast, and they turn up their noses, as though you're nothing more than a pesky nuisance who's been hounding them since the day they were born, peddling that stuff that's so awful it might as well be strained chopped liver.

This, in case you're wondering, is what is known as a Weaning Moment. And if you've been looking for a way out of this relationship—the one where the baby is the snacker and you're the snackee—then you should take this moment to button up your blouse for good, throw out the nursing bras, and go out and invest in some round-bottomed cups that not even a baby can knock over. You're free!

Some babies, however, don't seem to have these epiphanies. Long after they're walking, eating solid food, and managing a cup, they shrewdly insist on holding all their feeding options open. You'll be sitting on the couch, and the kid will cruise by, catch a glimpse of you, and realize that a five-second sip of milk would be just the thing to fill an otherwise boring minute in her life.

"There comes a point when you feel you've turned into a twenty-four-hour diner," said my friend Cathy. "Except that you're the only thing on the menu and the tips are lousy."

Nursing a talker: Be careful what you call it

There's something you should know if you keep breast-feeding beyond flat-on-the-back infancy. One day your baby is going to learn to talk.

This is bad for only one reason. For a long time after they're talking, babies don't have a lot of subjects to cover. They hardly ever, for instance, want to discuss the World Series. Instead, their favorite discussions involve going around pointing out objects and earnestly telling people the names of them.

Guess which objects of yours they are going to want to talk about.

This is why—while you're still in the hospital, right after you have made the decision to call it poop—you also have to come up with a name for breast-feeding. And may I say that, although "breast-feeding" itself has a nice, authoritative, clean sound to it, no new talker is going to be able to manage its three syllables. You might want to go for something simpler.

My friend Julie didn't have this little talk with herself in time, and boy, was she sorry. She and her husband kept jokingly referring to breast-feeding as "giving the kid nipples," and then were stunned when their eighteen-month-old stood up in the grocery cart one afternoon and screamed, "I want nipples now!"

Several old people looked positively pale, and some teenagers were thrown into hysterics. Julie abandoned the cart of groceries and headed out to the car, so she and the baby could discuss her body parts in private.

For this reason it's best, when talking about breasts and their functions, if you can select words that hopelessly mislead and confuse the public. Our culture is a little mentally ill on the subject of older babies still getting nourishment from their mothers, and so you probably don't want somebody saying out loud, "Mother, I think it would be delightful to take a break now for breast-feeding, don't you?"—even if he could manage to pronounce the words.

Much better is if you have named it something so innocuous that when the kid shouts for it, others scratch their heads and depend on you to translate. My friend Kate wisely called it milkies, and when her children wanted it, she simply acted as though they must be referring to the milk at home in the refrigerator. Of course, a close observer might notice that she was also putting on additional clothing—quilted vests and layers of sweaters—while she was saying this. A baby trying to make herself understood is not averse to coming over and yanking all the buttons off her mother's blouse, just to make sure the point gets across.

I thought I was being smart in calling it what it is: nursing. "Do you want some nursing?" I'd say, and the kid would scramble up on my lap. But "nursing" is a hard word for a new mouth to manage, and it came out as "ninnies" when it was being ordered. As in: "I want your ninnies!"

This, I'm sorry, sounds vaguely obscene and causes the same consternation among the members of the public as, "Woman, take out your boobs and give me some milk!" Certainly it never fooled anyone for one second. One time, after an outburst from my child, an older woman at the bus stop said to me, "Don't tell me you're still trying to nurse that child—and you with hardly anything up there to begin with!"

My friend Ellie definitely had the right idea, which she claims she didn't even think up on purpose. She had no formal name for what she was doing, but, as it turned out, she'd be nursing her child, and then after a while say to him, "Do you want the other side?" She didn't even realize it had taken root in his head until one day when he said to Ellie that he wanted "eat side."

She was able to tilt her head in a charmingly perplexed way (while folding her arms across her chest, of course, just as a precaution), and no one ever knew what he meant.

That's what you want to strive for, when you're in front of an audience, you know: an air of charmed perplexity. Come to think of it, that's the attitude that's going to get you through many future moments of parenthood.

Weaning a toddler: Stories of bribes and manipulations

Babies are easy to wean, if you want to. I don't know why anybody would want to stop a baby from nursing and go back to the bottle system, but every now and then it turns out to be a good idea. Suppose, for instance, world peace depends on your flying to the Middle East to negotiate some treaties, and you can't find room for the Lac-Tote refrigerator in your carry-on bag. You might decide to stop nursing. Maybe.

If that happens to you, rest assured that you and the baby can work this out very amicably. You can simply say, "Oh, I forgot to tell you. There's an unwritten law requiring all babies over (insert age here) to get their nourishment from bottles," and a baby will just take you at your word, and you and your breasts can resume your regular lives together, a little saggier but wiser.

The occasional baby might protest a little and decide that the rubber nipple isn't quite as delicious as your own, but this is one of those times when it's just as well that she can't talk. After a while—a baby's attention span being about two and a half seconds—she'll decide that rubber nipple or not, she's got to get at that milk. You will never in your life have to have a conversation about it with her. Trust me.

But many of us go on nursing long past this period. After all, it's still quite convenient having the milk right on hand—and in fact, when they're toddlers, sometimes nursing them is one of the only ways of getting them to be still and stop dismantling the kitchen cabinets. And best of all, when they're settled down and nursing in your lap, you can sometimes actually complete a sentence without being interrupted.

Still, I should warn you that once they know how to talk, they do have an opinion on this weaning business. Sometimes you actually have to convince them that it's a

136

great idea to stop clawing at the front of you and getting milk from your body.

Distraction sometimes works. The baby comes over to nurse, and you say, "Wow! Look at that truck out the window!" Or you could say, "Good heavens! Who in the world are the Democrats going to get to run in the first district this fall?" You can really say anything at all. The trick is to make this so dramatic and convincing that a baby forgets that there even are such things as nursing and breasts, and perhaps even milk itself.

This works on maybe one baby in every two million, and even then, it only works for forty-five seconds. Then you are going to have to think up something else that must be thought about at that precise second. You may need to race to the toy box and start throwing things out of it. You may have to charge through the hall, pretending you're an ambulance on your way to rescue the stuffed animals. Heck, you may have to invent a reason to evacuate the house.

All of this will buy you another fifty-two seconds.

The next thing to try is to encourage the baby to eat something else. "How about a banana?" you say sweetly, while the little monster is screeching at you and ripping the buttons off your blouse and they're popping all over the kitchen floor like jumping beans. "Some ice cream? How about the kitty food that you've always wanted so badly?"

No, no, no. You're never supposed to let things get to this point. If distraction hasn't worked, and the banana you offered has been hurled back at your face, then it is time to go into a serious rethinking of how you're going to wean this child. This is when everybody I know found themselves desperately thumbing through how-to books about babies. The best advice there is that you must have missed the Weaning Moment when the kid was eight months old and bored with you.

"Good God!" you say, banging your head on the wall. "Why didn't I see? Why did I let myself talk on the phone that afternoon when I'm sure he decided he didn't want to ever nurse again? Damn it!"

Don't blame yourself. We've all been there. I think baby-care books would do a great service if they would just remind us in bold letters, every page or so, that hardly ever do you find a nursing college student. Even most fourth-graders wouldn't touch the stuff.

I decided to wean my oldest child one afternoon when he came into the living room where I was talking with a friend and said calmly, "I want croutons with my nursing today." He was two.

It was as though scales fell instantly from my eyes. Croutons with nursing? What was I, some sort of all-purpose salad bar? Today it would be croutons and nursing, but what about tomorrow? Marinara sauce? Ketchup? I could see that it wasn't going to be a real stretch until we got to the point where we had theme nursing. Perhaps Mexican night, with some crunchy tortilla chips and salsa on the side. Later on, maybe some stuffed mushrooms and crab cakes.

I went to the library and checked out books about weaning, all of which scolded me for missing that supposedly golden Weaning Moment. Now, the books sighed, you are in for a struggle.

I decided it was time for desperate measures. The next day I told him that I had a feeling that the nursing milk had gone bad. "I just have a funny feeling about the milk," I said. "I think it doesn't taste good anymore."

"Oh, it's good," he said.

"Not anymore. Something happened to the milk today, and it's going to taste bad when you nurse before going to sleep."

"I still try," he said and went back to pushing his truck along the rug.

That night, I put him in his room and ran downstairs and put vinegar on my nipples. Okay, it sounds crazy, but some other hapless mother had told me that vinegar would curdle the milk and make it taste absolutely horrible. "He'll never want to nurse again," she promised.

"Boy, this milk is going to be terrible!" I said when I got back upstairs. "Peee-yooo. It's bad!"

He looked a little nervous when he latched on, but then he pulled away and looked at me, giving me what I now know was his most reassuring look. "It's okay. It taste like salad."

With my second child, I also missed the wonderful Weaning Moment. I do not know what is wrong with me that I just keep nursing through those what-is-this-chopped-liver-you're-trying-to-pass-off-on-me phase. But this time, here I was with a three-year-old who seemed determined to make a career of foraging for breast milk.

She was so old that she and I even had rational discussions about why it might not be such a good lifetime plan to keep nursing for so long. I even confided to her my deep feelings of dislike about being a snacking service. We worked out compromises: no drive-by nursing sessions— only the ones after waking up or just before going to sleep. No ripping at clothing, or mentioning nursing in public. You know, the basic rules.

But there came the day when I really did start to wonder about the college dean, and I said to her, "What would it take to get you to stop nursing?"

She said quickly, as though she'd been waiting for this question all her life: "A Strawberry Shortcake baby."

I am not ashamed to say that we got right in the car at that minute and drove to the toy store, where she picked out a Strawberry Shortcake baby and I happily wrote the check. All the way home I told her that whenever she felt like nursing, she could get out the Strawberry Shortcake doll and cuddle her. She could even come and cuddle with me, in fact—I wasn't trying to be heartless here and we might even play a game together.

"But," I said, "now you have this doll, and we've made a deal. No more nursing."

That night, we put her to bed with the baby doll tucked beside her, and I made a speech about how grown-up she was, and how proud I was of her.

At eleven that night, she came downstairs and stood in the doorway, looking at me. "I want nursing again," she said.

So I went back over the terms of the agreement once more. "No, no," she said happily, coming and settling in my lap. "It's okay now, because I threw the baby in the trash can."

With my third child, one day when she was two years old and asking to nurse, I said very firmly, "Oh, didn't I tell you? We don't do that anymore. You're too old now."

She said, "Oh," and went off to do something else.

The Weaning Moment at last.

Chapter 10:
Smashed Bananas and Cracker Paste

There's a reason they call it "solid" food

If you're dreading the moment you have to feed your baby actual human food, this is because at some point in your life you've probably seen someone who has just finished feeding an infant. There's no mistaking the applesauce-in-the-eye look, the strained peas dripping off the cheekbones, the bright orange carrot bits stuck in the hair. It's hard to want this in your own life.

The first question everybody wants answered is, *When do I actually have to start doing this?*

And of course, everyone you consult, including the mailman, has his own answer to this question. Some people act as though they believe babies should get their first solid food in utero if possible, but since it's not possible, then the absolute latest should be in the delivery room. They seem to think that, if only you'd planned ahead, you could have had a pizza sent to the delivery room so the kid could start getting used to anchovies.

Other, more moderate types won't start pestering you about starting pablum until you make the mistake of complaining that your newborn isn't yet sleeping through the night. These people believe that when babies cry in the middle of the night, they are really crying for rice cereal that has been ground into a dust-like consistency.

Once, when I asked a pediatrician when was a good time to start giving a baby solid food, she said you knew the baby was ready when he reached over and grabbed a chicken bone out of your hand and started beating you with it. I didn't ask her how vegetarians are supposed to know when to start. Presumably their babies grab a handful of tofu and grind it into their mother's hair.

Babies aren't usually very subtle when they've decided they want something. Once, in a restaurant, my friend Linda discovered her nine-month-old daughter was surreptitiously getting lettuce from a little boy at the next table. Linda wasn't sure how the two of them had worked out this deal, but by the time she discovered the transaction, the little boy's bowl was mostly empty. The next time Linda took her to the pediatrician and was asked what the baby was eating these days she replied, "Well, actually just breast milk and salad with Italian dressing."

The pediatrician nodded solemnly and said it might be a good idea to hold off for a while on the blue cheese or parmesan peppercorn.

Most babies take to solid foods quite readily, because even though they are new to the planet, they instantly grasp the idea that food has a lot of potential beyond simply providing nourishment, which, frankly, they couldn't care less about. It's more the weaponry aspect of food they find interesting, as well as the decorating possibilities.

As with so many other parenthood experiences, however, if you have invested in the correct paraphernalia, the dangerous effects can be ameliorated. In this case, you will need the food, of course, and a baby-sized spoon (preferably with some cartoon character on the end of it, although this character will quickly be covered in the food substance and won't be seen by your little one), a full-length plastic outfit and hood for yourself (a rain poncho and boots will do), the equivalent of a shower curtain for the floor, and a molded plastic suit of armor for the child. It is also helpful if you can move the high chair outdoors, close to where the hose is. If this is not feasible—say it's thirty degrees outside or there's a tornado going on—then your main goal should be to move the high chair as far away from the wallpaper as you can. And if you didn't have the foresight to install a drain in your floor, now is going to be the time you kick yourself for that.

As a safety measure, before feeding a baby, you should make sure you're wearing clothes that you don't care about—clothes that you would wear if you thought you might be witnessing a building demolition, for instance. Remove all jewelry and wristwatches, tie your hair back with a plain elastic band (no bangs), and then wrap yourself up in the poncho and hood. With some babies, it's a good idea to wear safety goggles—the sort that a person working with flying molten steel might wear.

You are ready to begin.

Keep this in mind at all times: A baby being given the choice of swallowing a bite of strained beets or catapulting it out of his mouth is going to go for the sensual choice, swishing it around for a few seconds and then sending it right back into space. Happily, not all of it will land on the chandelier or on your poncho. Some will remain on the baby. Your job will then be to take the baby-sized spoon and mop up his chin, which is now coated with strained beets, and try to reinsert them. (You are permitted to take a break to get any of the beets off your safety goggles that may be interfering with your ability to see the baby.)

Many experienced parents learn a complicated ducking maneuver as they insert a bite into the mouth, and then they resurface in time to drive the spoon all around the baby's chin and mouth area, like a backhoe bulldozing beets back into a hole. With a really creative baby, you might have to drive the spoon miles and miles around the chin before the spoon can gain entrance to the mouth again. Some babies realize right away that all they have to do is clamp their mouths shut, and you can't get the spoon inside.

This is when silly noises really come in handy. The way it works is this: You make a ridiculous noise—think barnyard animals after some hallucinogens, for instance—and the baby smiles, and bam! You reinsert the chin-recycled food.

Naturally a certain amount of these reinserted beets will find their way back onto the chin, and you will have to drive the spoon around again.

Don't be surprised if it takes more than ten minutes to get one spoonful of beets actually past the tongue. Some babies can play this game all day long, extruding beets in your direction and then squirming and batting your hand away while you try to get them to swallow.

You win if you get more than one-quarter of a teaspoon into them at any point—and they win if the opposite wall has at least two globs of food on it at the end of the feeding.

Then you bring in the hose.

Foods that any baby can turn into a paste product
Babies manufacture paste. This—although you hardly ever hear people mentioning it as the reason they wanted kids—is one of the chief advantages of having an infant around the house. It is certainly one of their best by-products. I think that babies have some special substance in their drool that bonds with practically anything. In case you've ever wondered why you hardly ever find parents of infants out buying glue, mucilage, or paste, that's why. They get all they need from the baby.

I used to think that Baby Paste only came from crackers and cereals mixed with saliva. But now I've noticed that some very wonderful, innovative adhesives are being produced these days from smashed-up vegetables and fruits. The advantage of these, from the baby's standpoint, is that they come in a variety of colors and consistencies. The glue that can be made with bananas or strained carrots, for instance, is quite dramatic. Some tots are doing wonders working in the medium of strained meat products that come in the jars, although most discriminating toddlers prefer to work with something with a little texture, like pieces of bologna or hot dogs. (Some of us don't like to give babies meats with nitrites, but in all fairness, it has to be said that the nitrites don't seem to interfere with the adhesive quality of the food.)

The most startling thing about these glue products—after you've finished marveling at their ability to withstand even the most vigorous rubbing and scraping—is how they are absolutely everywhere in your house. I think people contemplating having children should be told outright: First there's the Year of Pregnancy, Delivery, and Hardly Any Sex, and that is followed by the Year That Your House Has Baby Paste Everywhere.

You naturally expect to see this stuff on the coffee table, on the underside of every doorknob, and smeared all along the floorboards of the kitchen. You'd be a fool to think that any spot where a cruising baby can reach could go unadorned with Baby Paste. But why, you will one day be asking yourself, why is there this stuff on the package of light bulbs on the top kitchen shelf? Why do the family toothbrushes all have it stuck to the bristles, for God's sake? And you can't help but shudder, getting into bed at night, to find it coating your pillow and the alarm button on the clock radio.

There are some nights when Baby Paste seems to be creeping all over the house, like a sinister vine. You just know if you close your eyes to go to sleep, you might wake up in the morning to find your eyelids have been glued together. But who's kidding whom? There's no way you'll sleep through the night anyhow. Now that you think of it, maybe that's all for the best. Perhaps Nature doesn't have babies sleep through the night so that parents will have to wake up every few hours to make sure everybody's eyelids haven't been melded with Baby Paste.

The stuff that comes in jars

The best thing about baby food in the jars is that once the pesky food is gone, the jars are great for storing buttons, tacks, safety pins, nails, and anything else that's been cluttering your family's various junk drawers. And, oh yes, jarred baby food does keep you from having to worry about what to feed the baby. You just go look in the cabinet and say, "Okay, kid, it's strained English peas for dinner tonight. We've got three jars of the stuff."

My friend Pam says you never feel as secure as you do when you open up the cabinet and see stacks and stacks of baby food jars, all containing green, brown, and yellow substances. They just shout out Nutrition!

They may be shouting about nutrition all they want from behind the cabinet door, but once on the face of the baby, food from the jar is going to look more like clown makeup than anything edible. And it looks even worse on you. So little of the stuff actually gets inside the baby that some people have decided they'd save money by grinding up their own food.

This sounds like a great idea. After all, the baby gets the kind of food you eat, which gets her accustomed to what's in store for her when she's grown some teeth. You wouldn't dream of eating canned spinach, so why foist it off on some unsuspecting kid just because that person can't talk yet to complain? And it's so easy, too: You just take out the blender and press one of the fourteen buttons, and presto! You have enough baby food to feed Portugal.

Of course, this will eventually get to be a problem, because you don't have enough places to store food for Portugal. And since you don't manufacture those handy little glass jars, you'll have to stack all of it in your refrigerator, which will lead you right into yet another circle of Leftover Hell. It's even worse than the Leftover Hell you're already living in, mainly because you'll open plastic refrigerator dishes of strained vegetables and not be able to tell if the orange fuzz is actual mold or if it's simply strained carrots mixed in with strained beef stew.

No sugar, salt, preservatives: Food perfectionism

There's something about the perfection of babies— the way their skin and hair seem so unspoiled and smell so good—that makes people think they can keep them that way just by making sure no horrible stuff ever gets into their mouths.

My friend Jeanne would talk for hours about how her newborn baby wasn't ever going to have candy, not even once in his whole life. There would be none of that dreadful chemical-laden icing on his birthday cakes. Hell, there might not even be any birthday cakes. No salt either, or modified cornstarch. And at the mention of preservatives, Jeanne would pick up the baby and hold him protectively to her chest, as if preservatives were floating in the air and she had to shield him with her very body.

"I just think of his sparkling clean, pink colon, and I know I don't want to be the person who corrupts it with bad stuff," she said once.

We, her friends who had seen the way toddlers can put away a bowl of dried-up cat food when no one is looking, pointed out that this was probably excessive worry on her part, and that she might want to seek help.

Wanting to protect your kid's gastrointestinal tract from the food that everyone else is constantly eating is probably a very noble idea, but if you are to live a rich and full life, you must discard this notion right away. The thing to remember is that life is already very hard, and the brain damage you're suffering from sleep and sex deprivation may prevent you from being able to carry out such a bold plan. The day will come when you're holding a screaming, hungry baby and staring at a cabinet full of soy grits and uncooked whole wheat pasta—and the next thing you know, you'll be grinding up Cheez Whiz and saltines in the blender, and pouring RC Cola into the Playtex nurser.

Remember this: You can't sustain life on any food that you have to stir for twenty minutes, only to have it resemble wallpaper paste when you're through. A baby will live on that stuff for a while, but one day you'll be with him in the park and he'll come wandering over, chewing on an old Band-Aid he found in the sandbox, thinking this is the most delicious flavor he's ever tasted.

Besides used Band-Aids, you might as well know that other foods on the All-Time Baby Hit Parade include:

- Dirt—the browner and wormier the better. Beach sand and sandbox sand are also wildly popular, particularly in clumps.
- Grass clippings. (This is a baby's favorite vegetable.)
- Previously chewed gum found on the undersides of public tables and chairs.
- Houseflies from the windowsills. (A good protein source.)
- The stuffing inside teddy bears. (Known in nutritional circles as roughage.)
- The first page of your tax return and your W-2 forms.
- Dog food.

Spaghetti goes on the head; that's why it's made in strands

There's hardly a kid in America who doesn't instinctively know to upturn her bowl of spaghetti on top of her head. I think it should be listed with the Academy of Pediatrics as a developmental milestone, in fact.

Doctors' appointments should go like this.

Doctor: Is she rolling over yet?

Parent: Oh, yes. Backwards and forwards.

Doctor: Good. How many teeth?

Parent: Four.

Doctor: Does she make a decent Cheerios paste?

Parent: We're finding the stuff all over the place.

Doctor: Let me ask you this. How long since you've had to buy any glue?

Parent: Oh, not since she was three months old.

Doctor: And spaghetti. Does she put spaghetti on her head?

Parent: All the time.

Doctor: Good. I think things are coming along nicely.

Babies instantly see all the possibilities of food. Why eat it when that means it will simply be gone? Not only do they immediately know that spaghetti strands had to be designed to go on top of the head, but carrots—which resemble crayons—are most certainly meant for writing on the walls. To a baby, the possibilities are endless: Pudding was intended to be a kind of shampoo, and peas are obviously ballistic devices, designed to be blown out of the mouth with the goal of hitting the chandelier. And all brown and green foods—I'm sure you've noticed this temptation in your own life—are clearly to be ground up with the hands and smeared on every surface within reach.

Occasionally you may look around your house and become concerned that there is so much food on every available surface that surely none has actually gotten into your child. In fact, you will see that somehow there is more food all over your walls and floors than you have even purchased at the store. Ever. Pediatricians are used to hearing about this from parents. One of their most important functions—after saving lives—is to reassure parents that their babies are getting enough to eat.

It's really one of my very favorite speeches of all the talks they give. You call up, near hysteria, because you have not seen one discernible piece of food pass through your child's mouth in so many days you can't even count them, and your pediatrician tells you, in a calm and placating tone, that he's quite sure that if your baby is pooping and peeing, she is getting enough to eat.

"Is she having bowel movements and urinating regularly?" he will ask you. He uses the medical terms just to let you know that he's on duty and not taking this lightly.

Well, of course any baby is doing that stuff. That's her main activity. So when you admit that yes, you are still changing an incredible number of diapers, the pediatrician will launch into a wonderful little talk about how babies— when left to their own devices—will actually balance their own diets. This, although it cannot be true in a world in which there are potato chips and Cheez Whiz, is one of those beliefs that you will not be able to shake your pediatrician from holding. It is similar to their notion that babies eventually do sleep.

If you are still hysterical, the doctor will say, "To make yourself feel better, why don't you write down a list of everything your baby eats in the next twenty-four hours? You'll see that it's pretty much a balanced diet."

I actually did this one time. I followed my sixteen-month-old daughter around and watched her all day long. In the end, I had to admit the pediatrician was technically correct: Besides the three houseflies I'm pretty sure she ate off the windowsill, she had eaten six raisins, one string bean, and the electric bill.

When I told the pediatrician this, he thought a bit more protein than houseflies might be a good idea. "Maybe try a couple of slices of turkey," he suggested kindly.

Not many people probably would be willing to tell their doctors about the insect-eating, but I feel that it's important for them to get bulletins from the real world occasionally. After all, they have to work a zillion hours a day—so even if they do have their own children, they never see them. You can bet their nannies aren't telling them the truth about the stuff their kids really eat day after day.

I'll bet the average pediatrician thinks his kids are getting three well-balanced meals a day, and even nodding off to sleep in their own beds. I've been tempted several times, when faced with Pediatric Theory, to ask for their home phone numbers so I could consult with their nannies.

To the nanny, I could tell the real truth. Not only was it three houseflies, but I think dessert might have been a wad of chewing gum my child found stuck to the bottom of a chair at the car wash—and she got her minerals for the day from licking some rocks she found in the parking lot.

Chapter 11: On Their Planet, Shoes Were Gods

Dressing a baby

There's really nothing complicated about dressing a baby—once you've grasped the concept that their heads really aren't connected to their necks as well as other people's are. You will quickly realize, the first time you try to put a T-shirt on a baby, that you are lacking approximately four of the hands you would need to accomplish this. Nothing you've done until now in your life has prepared you for this moment.

The second you try to put the shirt over the baby's head, the kid will start shrieking to anyone within five miles that you're trying to smother her. (Babies are very paranoid about the idea that somebody might try to smother them; this seems to be something they learned in the womb, where—although the accommodations you created were very nice—there still was not a whole lot of air, through no fault of your own.)

When you try to get their heads into the neck of some piece of clothing that the garment industry seemed to think appropriate for babies, you'll be shocked to see that not only do their heads flop around like crazy, but it seems that they're also about five times the size of the neck opening, no matter what size clothing you buy. Babies hate it when you try to force their heads through neck holes, because it makes them remember that horrendous day when they were trying to get themselves propelled out of you. That whole day was just one gigantic, squeezing turtleneck, from their point of view, and what baby is going to willingly relive that experience so soon after? Therefore, they think they need to scream and flop around and bat at you with their little fists, and you can just see that they're thinking, "Oh my God, I can't go through one more second of this! I fought my way out of this woman once—now does she expect me to do it every damn day?" (It's a little known fact that American babies come equipped with all the usual swearwords.)

In the next few months, however, you are going to get to be quite a professional at juggling the baby's massive head, the shirt, and the flailing limbs—both yours and the baby's—and be able to wrestle the kid into an outfit, with just a few deft maneuvers and only minimal swearing from you or the baby. The first time you do it, however, I would advise that you make sure no other people are around, unless, of course, you can get some medics to agree to stand outside the door, just in case one of you needs CPR before the ordeal is over.

Baby fashion statements

Once you get the baby home from the hospital, you have a momentous decision to make. I know this is tough, right on the heels of having to accept your incompetence at taking adorable baby photographs and mailing them, but you have to do it. You must sit down and take a good look at your baby and decide if your child is preppy, grunge, or a person who looks nice in friendly farmyard animals.

For years, babies were pretty much relegated to wearing clothing that had ducks and bunnies all over it. For some reason, the garment industry had taken a stand on the issue and felt that small, defenseless children should be attired in pictures of small, nonthreatening animals. I think it was mostly by default that babies got stuck with this stuff: Who else, the fashion industry mused, was going to wear such things?

Parents went along with this too, I'm afraid. We were all too tired to care much. More times than I can count, I've gone running to the Sears baby department to buy something for the kid to wear, and I have never once stood there and said, "My God, what is it with these cute, nonthreatening animals all over everything? Why can't I find something in a reptile pattern?"

I didn't even wonder why babies couldn't dress like everyone else. That's how little imagination I had for baby fashion. The first time I saw a baby in a pair of faded blue jeans—the standard Levi's kind, with five pockets and zippers and rivets—I laughed for a week. I was slow to catch on to the idea that this was what the world had been waiting for.

But these days there is no reason for a baby not to be a perfect Imitation Adult. There are baby Calvin Klein jeans and brand-name sneakers. There are baby khakis and pinstripes. They can wear plaid flannel shirts with leggings. There are pleated skirts, penny loafers, and boat shoes. There are baby tuxedoes, for God's sake. And if your three-week-old baby girl should get asked out to a formal dinner, for instance, there are no doubt baby evening gowns with sequined slippers out there.

Sometimes life is so hysterical and ridiculous that these clothes will actually make sense to you. You'll find yourself in a store, pawing at the baby tuxedo-and-cummerbund ensemble, and you will desperately want to see your own dear child wearing it, the $175 be damned. You will want it because it is there, because it is possible, and yes, because the baby can't stop you.

Do not, under any circumstances, do this to your kid.

Oh, sure, you might get a few laughs for yourself. There is something hysterically funny about an eighteen-inch-long person doing that William Frawley impression that is so popular with babies, and wearing a size zero tuxedo, that it will make you fall down on the ground laughing. I mean, you are not going to be able to stand it, it's going to be so hilarious. You'll be wetting your pants and screaming. You'll be wetting the couch and screaming.

But I ask you this: Will you truly respect yourself for this kind of behavior? Will you feel comfortable showing the kid the pictures of him done up this way, once he's old enough to call the lawyers?

The nudist years

Once babies figure out that you're putting clothing on their bodies, they start wanting to take it off. This does not happen overnight. For the longest time, they can't quite figure out what it is that you're doing to them, why several times a day, you haul them over to the changing table and start bothering them with unsnapping and resnapping, shoving their arms and legs back and forth and generally making a nuisance of yourself. They think it's just one more of the bizarre things about you. Even though they're required by the Baby Regulations to yell and squirm and protest, they don't quite get it that you're actually redecorating them.

But then one day it occurs to them that all this clothing stuff is optional. It's not attached. You can almost see this dawning on them, their little eyes lighting up with the realization that these ducks and bunnies aren't, in fact, part of their anatomy.

They grab onto a bootie and hurl it experimentally off into space. This moment, you might as well know, is the official beginning of the nudist years.

By the time they are fifteen months old, they'll know everything there is to know about getting out of their clothes.

You'll come to fetch them out of their crib in the morning to find the diaper has been flung to the other side of the room, along with the sopping-wet pajamas, the crib bumpers, and any stuffed animals that were within range.

Out in the world, it's the same thing. Turn your head away for one minute, and when you turn back, there is going to be a little naked person sitting in front of you. You can try to thwart them by buying them clothing that has complicated fasteners—all located in the back—but keep in mind that they're members now of a toddler nudist network. Whenever one toddler realizes that another is dressed and doesn't wish to be, he is right there to aid in the unfastening.

Some people choose to fight with their babies about clothing removal, but I frankly don't think you have the energy to triumph on this one. You might as well take a Zen view of the problem. Your task will be to repeatedly put the baby back in his pinstripe shirt and khaki pants, and his equally important task will be to elude you and get naked. He will eventually learn to stash his clothes in places where they are not so easy to find, and run through the house, giggling and naked, while you search for his clothes. Take deep breaths, and try to be thankful for every moment he's not peeing into the houseplants.

Clothing No Self-Respecting Baby Can Wear

- Bibs. Babies are required by statute to pull and tug at a bib until it comes off, making as many choking noises as possible.
- Hats. No hat shall ever be tolerated on a baby, no matter what the season. Bald babies have to be especially diligent that parents don't try to hide the top of their heads.
- Socks and shoes. These, fortunately, are easily accessible to babies, even though sometimes it's tough to untie those freaking bows and knots.

- Anything frilly or with lace on it. These types of clothing must be spit up on immediately. Not projectile vomiting, of course, since it's difficult to aim. A nice dribbly spit-up should do.
- Any clothing with cute sayings on it, such as "I'm precious" or "Daddy's Little Angel." It's important for a baby to scream and cry incessantly if she finds herself in these, to disprove once and for all any assumptions strangers might make.

Dressing up for shock: Why do boys always love the gold lame?

We live in mostly enlightened times. Men get to wear pink shirts, ponytails, and earrings to work, something that only women could legally do several years ago. And since there's a trickle- down effect, we're now seeing boys being allowed to have dolls (okay, so they call them Action Figures) and sleep with cuddly stuffed animals, as long as they're called Beanie Babies. But for some reason, let a boy toddle over to the housekeeping corner of his day-care center and put on a bridal veil, and whoa! People start sending out for counselors.

Kids live for that stuff. A little boy isn't sure what just happened that made you start quaking and made your eyes bug out, but the next time you look over, he's added the gold lame evening gown and some T-strap high-heeled sandals you'd die for, if only they were in your size. And he's giving you his best wide-eyed grin.

That's because kids have built-in Shock Detectors. It's one of their most important features, installed at the baby factory before you even met them. When they see you clutching your heart and groping to find a chair, they're delighted to replay the scene for you over and over again.

Some people think you should try to ignore what you don't want them to do, but I don't know anybody who's had great success with this plan, except one woman whom I suspect had a lobotomy or else is always on heroin. If you really can't bear the idea of your two-year-old son wearing a French maid's costume and trying to breastfeed the day-care dolls, then you may have to develop a talent for suddenly leaving the room. Either that, or you could try to get some psychotherapy for yourself, but how in the world are you going to find the time for that?

Besides, just as soon as you get your head and heart enlightened on this question, the phase will pass, and some new shocker will take its place. Next he'll be wanting to wear nothing but camouflage face paint, and he'll pick up crayons and pretend they're Uzis that he's required to kill you with. You'll have to go back to your therapist and say, "Well, I guess we're not dealing with a cross-dresser, after all. it seems we've got a little psychokiller on our hands."

Lots of people are much more relieved at the thought of a psychokiller-in-training than a toddler in drag, you know. But the important thing to remember is that nothing that happens right now is liable to be permanent.

Go ahead; take a picture of him traipsing around in his bridal outfit. Years later, he won't remember that he ever wore it, and you can sell him the negatives to finance your old age in one of the finest nursing homes.

Mittens and hats in August, bathing suits in January

You knew, going into parenthood, that you would have lots of opportunities to quarrel about clothes. Surely you remember your own seventh-grade year, when you wanted to wear fishnet stockings and a fedora to school, and your mother thought that blue-and-white gingham dress looked so nice on you. What you may not remember, though, is that these clothing fights started back when you were two years old and insisted on wearing your wool hat with the ear flaps all summer long.

Right when the nudity phase starts subsiding, the wonderful world of seasonal clothing takes over. Only, it's always the wrong seasonal clothing. There's not a two-year-old in America who will tolerate wearing a snowsuit, except when it's ninety degrees outside and it's his personal idea to put it on. In the winter, of course, it takes a one-hundred-twenty-five-pound adult with a good amount of upper-body muscle mass to get a thirty-pounder into the average snowsuit. In our family, it often took two such adults—one for the top end of the kid and one for the bottom end—and even then, both of us were so exhausted afterwards that we had to call 911 for a couple of ambulances.

I once took my two-year-old daughter to the beach for the day, and watched as she tried, wretchedly, to build a sand castle while wearing wet and muddy Winnie-the-Pooh mittens. I could see by the looks other people were giving me that I was suspected of being the kind of insidious child abuser that would devise this as a punishment for an ordinary, angelic little toddler. People seemed concerned every time I spoke to my child, as though next I might suggest that we leave the beach and head for a tattoo parlor for mother-daughter tattoos. I kept trying to smile good-naturedly at everyone, just to show what kind of lovable person I really am.

"Honey, don't you want to take off your mittens?" I would inquire loudly, every now and then, just so people would know I still had all my faculties.

"No!" she would scream. "No look at my hands!"

This did no good to my reputation. By the time we left the beach, she was crying to go home and get her winter boots.

I know that a lot of people would think that a reasonably organized parent with storage space in her house should not have to be faced with these tough seasonal problems. I have had single, childless people say to me, with straight faces: "Why don't you simply put the off-season clothing away, for God's sake?" This is just another reason why, once you have a baby, your life as a single person seems very distant and far away. You dimly remember that you once did manage to put the off-season clothing away. Now that you're a parent, it seems that you must have missed that five-minute period when it was technically possible for you to make your way into the attic with a box of winter clothes. Probably you chose instead to go to the bathroom unaccompanied by your toddler.

Also, even if you did manage to get some of it up there, it's naive to assume that it's even possible to get rid of all the off-season clothing. Oh, sure, you can try. Go ahead and put it in the attic. Mail it to your mother in Florida. Stick it in your safe deposit box at the bank. There will still be your toddler, showing up for breakfast, wearing a pair of Mickey Mouse earmuffs and a woolen scarf. Don't ask how this could happen. I suspect that off-season clothing has a mind of its own. I know this because once I got up in the middle of the night to pee and discovered a wool watch cap sitting in the hallway. It was obviously making its midnight trek into the baby's room. It flattened itself against the wall and let me pass, unmolested, but I knew things could have gotten ugly if I'd attempted to send it back where it belonged.

You want to stay friendly with the off-season clothing if you can.

Red shoes with sparkles

Babies know a pair of sexy shoes when they see them. You may think you can get away with putting them in those sturdy, orthopedic-type white high-tops, but believe me, they look around and see that none of the cool people are wearing those. Almost as soon as they can hold their heads up, they want the hot red sandals and the patent leather Mary Janes. I have seen a baby learn to walk on the spot, just so she could get across the room to a shiny pair of black patent leather shoes with ankle straps.

And the thing about a baby's passion that's different from the way a grown-up feels about shoes is simple: When a baby is under the spell of a pair of shoes, she wants to wear them all the time, especially in the bathtub, to bed, and while splashing in the wading pool. Mostly, no matter how much I love a new pair of shoes, I'm still willing to go barefoot to bed at night.

But not one of my kids has ever agreed with me on that. We have instead worked on compromises: Instead of being on the feet during the sleep time, I suggest a comfy spot right next to the bed. This has never worked. The best deal I've been able to work out is to have the Beloved Footwear on the pillow. My diplomatic skills are not tip-top by the time bedtime chugs around. I'm also not proud of the fact that on many nights, I have had to read the shoes a story and then kiss them goodnight. Shoes are not good kissers.

Shoes No Toddler Can Resist

- Black patent leather Mary Janes that are waxed to such a gleam that you can look in them to floss your teeth.
- Bunny slippers, but only if the bunnies are so huge that the average baby can't see over the top.
- Puffy winter boots.
- Anything with a stiletto heel that no woman in her right mind would wear longer than thirty seconds.
- Pointy cowboy boots.
- Industrial-weight, insulated work boots.
- The actual shoes Dorothy wore in The Wizard of Oz.

As tough as it was for me to think up a goodnight story and then kiss the shoes, my friend Ellen had it much worse. Her sixteen-month-old son, Brian, fell in love with a pair of very sexy work boots. These were the kind of boots construction workers wear, so that in case whole houses fall down on their toes, it won't hurt. But Brian somehow came into possession of a pair in just his size, and right away he could see that this was a good look for him. He had sort of a Bruce Springsteen thing going that summer—just the plain white diaper, a curly lock of black hair, and then these devastating work boots. Ellen had to wait until he was in stage-four sleep every night so she could remove them, and half the time, even then, he woke up screaming, as though she were taking off his feet themselves with no anesthetic.

Ellen was naturally very worried about what would happen when Brian outgrew these boots. Would they have to be surgically removed, or would they just stunt his foot growth? All her friends used to ponder this. She started looking for a new pair months before Brian actually needed them, but then, wouldn't you know, once the old shoes started feeling too tight, he grew tired of his Springsteen thing and went off in another direction with some casually aristocratic Top-Siders.

It was too bad. For his second birthday, I bought him a denim diaper cover with an embroidered American flag and Born in the U.S.A. stenciled in, but it was no use. He had found a pair of khaki Bermuda shorts and a polo shirt, and he was ready to indulge his preppier side. I think Ellen was relieved, but I'd been looking forward to teaching him some air guitar.

If it's 2:30, it must be time for me to change into my PINK dress

Long before I had kids—or even thought about it— my friend Kathy would bring her two-year-old daughter, Alexis, over to my house. And if I couldn't turn off the stereo quickly enough and get into a hiding place, then I would spend a morning entertaining them.

First Kathy would unload two or three steamer trunks of Alexis's clothes from her van. Then she'd go back and get a suitcase full of shoes, a garbage bag filled to the top with hair accessories, and several purses filled with costume jewelry. I was able to accommodate these visits because I had the kind of bricks-and-boards and beanbag-chair-style graduate student furniture that could easily be moved outdoors until they went back home. Other people, Kathy confided, weren't so nice about moving their Drexel dining room sets out into their yards. Therefore, I got lots of visits.

I correctly surmised that Alexis was an unbelievable tyrant, but what I didn't know was that this is a two-year-old's main job—to run the world and to change clothes a lot. The three of us would sit together, all drinking apple juice and commenting on the weather, and then Alexis would leap to her feet and declare that she was wrongly dressed. It was time for something blue, she'd say.

"I want to look sweet," she'd claim. So there Kathy and I would be, like two doting stage mothers, fastening and unfastening outfits, putting up and putting down wispy baby hair, buckling and unbuckling shoes. Each time, Alexis would play for approximately five seconds—ten seconds was our goal—and then the process would start all over.

"It's like being in a very bad play with lots of costume changes," whispered Kathy. I noticed that Kathy always seemed to be wearing the same thing with each visit: a grubby pair of blue jeans and a grayish white T-shirt. "It's so weird that I get the kid who can't wear the same outfit for longer than a few nanoseconds—when I've never cared anything about clothes at all," she said once.

This is how you know there's a master plan at work, matching up babies and parents. How would it work if everybody in one family were changing all the time? Who would do the buttons?

Chapter 12:
You *Can* Leave Home Without Them

Babies are technically not anatomical attachments

Legally, as a person living in the United States of America, you are allowed to leave your child. You have the inalienable right to put on clothes that do not have spit-up on them and leave the house for whole minutes at a time. It doesn't seem possible, I know. At first, when you are out somewhere without your baby, you'll feel as though you've left home without some body part—say, your left arm or something. You'll look around in alarm every few moments, thinking, "Oh, my God! Where's that thing that's supposed to be attached to me? And how did it fall off?"

Then you'll remember that it's simply your baby you're accustomed to lugging around, and that the baby is perfectly safe at home, being cared for by someone else. If your sleep deprivation has been too great lately, you may have to work a little to remember just who is, in fact, taking care of the baby. Believe me, this effort will cause you many small moments of fright that will feel a lot like actual heart attacks.

My friend Linda used to worry that she would simply forget to hire a babysitter, and would one day walk out the front door and find herself, hours later, having a wonderful time and then realize that oh, yes, she was a mother now, and oh my God, had she really left the baby alone? She was forever having to stop and lean against buildings, clutching her chest while she made herself remember that yes, it was okay; her mother was with the baby.

This is one of those side effects of being a parent that nobody ever thinks to tell you about. You can leave home, but for the first few months, you might want to carry around some spare oxygen tanks just to prevent yourself from hyperventilating on the public streets. Or better yet, pin a note to yourself saying, "I am the parent of an infant. If I appear to be having a mini-stroke, please remind me politely that my mother is watching the baby today. Thank you."

Your first time out
The first time you go out alone should be relatively soon after giving birth. If your first time away from the baby is to look for an apartment for her, then you have obviously waited too long. It is good to practice on short trips at first, just to make sure you still remember how to interact with adults in public settings. It's hard to remember in the beginning that it's not incumbent upon you to whip out your breast, for instance, whenever you hear other people's children wailing in the distance, just because your milk decides to start flowing. Also, it's good to practice standing still, without swaying back and forth, the way you find you automatically do when you're holding your baby.

Naturally, the entire time you are out, you are going to feel weird. It's a little like being an escapee from a prison. You keep expecting everyone who comes up to you to see by the hollows of your eyes and the way you now shuffle when you walk that you're actually an escaped inmate, and they'll send you off somewhere.

I went to lunch with a group of friends when my first child was four days old. I didn't want to, mind you; I wasn't even hungry for lunch, but my mother-in-law insisted that I go. She said I needed to spend some time with other people. She said it would be good for the baby to realize other people could take care of him, not that he was conscious of such things yet. Actually, I could tell that she was sick of me saying things to her like, "That's not the way to hold a baby... and please try not to drop him on the floor. We've decided we're never ever going to allow him to get dropped."

So I went and sat in a restaurant with three women who didn't have any children, and the whole time we were there, I kept noticing that they wanted to talk about the most boring things in the world. I had never noticed until that day what trivial people I had been hanging out with. One woman wanted to talk about politics, for God's sake. Another thought she might have the answers to world hunger. (I forget just what her solutions were. I remember being amazed that breast milk didn't figure into any of them.)

I sat there, blinking in the light like somebody who'd been chained up by kidnappers in the basement for the last ten years. I simply could not believe that waiters bustled around, dishes were served, people were going in and out of office buildings, and that all around me, stupid, meaningless conversations were being held. Not once did the talk turn to the miraculous invention of the pacifier or even the average length of time it takes an episiotomy to heal.

Finally, when it seemed imperative to contribute something to the conversation, I told everyone I had decided to go with a diaper service rather than disposable diapers, even though it meant buying lots of rubber diaper covers, and of course, having to rinse out diapers in the toilet. The diaper service, I explained reasonably, didn't want to take away diapers with actual objects in them.

"Still," I said, "although rinsing the diaper in the toilet is sort of gross if you stop and think about it, the poops really aren't so bad as long as the baby is nursing. In fact, the poops are really quite sweet smelling."

One of my so-called friends looked away.

166

"You know, they're not all brown and stinky like other people's," I said. "They're kind of yellow. Like mustard almost."

"Isn't that great?" said another of the women. I noticed she had pushed her plate away, and that she had been eating a ham sandwich, which was oozing mustard.

"No, no," I said. "Not like table mustard at all. It's quite sweet. It smells like—sort of like—"

"Really," said one of the women. "I'll pay you a thousand dollars if you won't tell us what baby shit smells like."

Many months later, I heard that they had decided not to invite me out again until the kid was in college.

Picking a sitter

When you're looking for a sitter for your baby, be warned: Everyone looks like a hired killer. Just when you're looking at people in a whole new context—is this a person who can be trusted not to set the sofa on fire?—suddenly it seems the news each night is filled with tales of nannies throwing babies out with the trash, and daycare centers sending one-year-olds out to play on the highway. No one seems safe. Even your mother can't produce the credentials you need to make sure she won't go on a rampage and start hacking away at your dining room furniture and letting hitchhikers come in to paint obscenities on the walls. I mean, you think she probably won't, but can she prove it?

That's the major question. Who can prove anything? When you're looking for a sitter, life comes into stark focus as just what it is: unpredictable, dangerous, and ultimately fatal. As if the scales have been ripped from your eyes, you see that you have insanely and recklessly brought a child into the world—and now all of life is going to conspire to show you what a ridiculous leap of faith that was.

What's ironic is that just a few short weeks ago, you felt totally incompetent taking care of this newborn infant. Now you see that you are a freaking genius compared to anyone else you might leave her with.

Meanwhile, all your friends are telling you that you and your spouse have got to get out of the house for a date with each other. People who have never cared one whit about your social life with your husband are now calling you up to tell you how important it is to "connect as a couple."

"We did connect as a couple," my friend Kathy finally told one of her overly concerned friends. "That's how we got into this mess in the first place."

I frankly do not see what the big deal is about going out. You'll be lucky if one of you doesn't fall unconscious into the pasta. And even if you should manage to stay awake, do you know the kind of conversation you're likely to be having?

You: Would you pass the, uh, the—you know—

What's-his-name: The what?

You: The stuff. You know, the white stuff—

What's-his-name: Baby powder? I don't think I remembered to bring the baby powder—

You: No, not baby powder! Why would I want baby powder in the restaurant? I want the white stuff that goes on food. Why were you thinking of baby powder? Are you thinking about calling home?

What's-his-name: How should I know why I was thinking about baby powder? It's the only white stuff, besides spit-up, that I've seen in a month.

You: The baby is probably spitting up on the sitter right now. We should call home.

What's-his-name: I think we just called home five minutes ago.

You: Yes, but now there's a reason. The sitter might be able to remember what you call the white stuff that goes on food. (Rummaging through purse for cellular phone.) Oh, wait, I think it's salt!

What's-his-name: (Rising in alarm.) I thought babies shouldn't have salt.

This is not what your friends have in mind for you. They're thinking romance—or sex—which is a laughable idea when you've just had a kid. If you got anywhere near a bed out on a date, you'd go right to sleep. It's best that you even avoid furniture showrooms for a long time after having a baby.

Still, the time is going to come when you need to get out. Trust me: You will want to see a movie without someone slurping on your breast during it. Maybe you will even want someone to bring you food at a nice table somewhere—a table that doesn't have a baby seat propped on top of it. You will like the idea of changing out of your nightgown and putting aside the cans of Chef Boyardee ravioli that you've been living on, and venturing out in public with regular people.

To do this, you will have to talk one of your relatives into coming to sit with the kid, or you will have to hire an actual sitter. This is just a night out, remember, so you won't need a full personality profile, IQ tests, and bank records for this person. However, the more you listen to the news and talk to other people, the more it seems that most prospective sitters are the kind of people who like to snack on house pets and who probably don't have a reflection when they look in the mirror.

Here, in case you're losing perspective, is a list of people that it's probably okay to leave your baby with—after the standard reference check, that is.

- Your best friend. (You're going to have to forget about the times she got drunk, including the time she poured vodka in the fish tank.)
- Your mother and mother-in-law.

- A trained nurse practitioner, particularly one with pediatric experience.
- An actual pediatrician.
- Someone who has brought more than one child to exemplary adulthood. (You can ask to see diplomas, notes from coaches, college professors, or U.S. senators to prove it.)
- A person hired by most of your friends, particularly if this person has not been involved in any child-selling scams.

If it will make you feel better, you're allowed to put sitters through any employment interview you can think of. My friend Jeanne, who required Pre-Babysitting Meetings with all her prospective sitters, once drew up a detailed personal history form for them to fill out. She told me later that some people actually get a little huffy when you want to see five credit references, their elementary school report cards, and documents proving they are legally sane. Jeanne said she weeded out the bad ones simply by asking if they'd mind getting fingerprinted at the police station before showing up for the interview.

Naturally the ones who balked at this didn't get hired because they were obviously hiding something—and the ones who already had fingerprints at the police station were definite criminals. Sometimes Jeanne decided not to hire the ones who agreed to be fingerprinted, because she felt they were so eager for the job that they were probably psychopathic killers, desperate to get to her child. Jeanne didn't get out much for a long time.

That won't happen to you. After all, the world really is full of nice people—many of whom are capable of taking care of your baby for a few hours so you can go to a movie or out to dinner. You will find one of them. It helps to ask friends with children for names of people they've hired, and then invite the sitter over to meet the baby and have a cup of tea just to see if she seems competent. Somebody who spills the cup of tea all over the rug won't be a good option.

Keep in mind, though, that leaving home will never be easy again. For one thing, you now have to leave a detailed list of things you think the sitter needs to know.

Here are some things you might want to include.

List of Things Your Sitter Needs to Know

- Your baby's name, social security number, and blood type, and location of main pacifier.
- A list of the places you'll be, along with telephone numbers.
- A handy chart showing how to diaper and clean the baby, in case this person might not know which end the diaper normally goes on.
- A list of everything your baby has done all day long, including naps, meals, and number of Cheerios flung under the table.
- A map with the setup of your kitchen, living room, bedrooms, and bathrooms. Mark the places where you suspect some extra pacifiers might be hiding.
- The baby book, in case she has time to enter some remarks.
- Detailed descriptions of all the things you do to get the baby to sleep. Include the specific speed for the stroller ride around the dining room table, the exact location on the baby's back where she is accustomed to being patted, the position she likes for rocking. If you sing lullabies, leave a copy of the lyrics and sheet music.
- The telephone numbers of the pediatrician, both of your mothers, the neighbors, a plumber, electrician, the poison control center, the landlord, and all your friends.

- A flashlight, batteries, transistor radio, bottled water, and a map to the emergency room.

The sitter for the long haul

This is a crazy idea, of course, as any veteran parent will tell you. Unless you have an unemployed mother who wants to take up full-time grandmotherhood, there is no such thing as the Sitter for the Long Haul, unless your hauls are very abbreviated indeed. But if your workplace is demanding that you come back to them or they will hire someone more competent, reliable, and with better birth control methods, then you are going to have to come up with someone who will pretend, for a while, at least, that she will take care of your baby every day while you go back to work.

Sitters really do plan to come every day when you first hire them. They don't know yet that taking care of babies is only bearable if you are the one who gave birth to them, if you are their grandparent, or have suffered a head trauma and have an unexplained desire to experience wailing sounds interspersed with horrific boredom.

Therefore, you are right to be suspicious of anyone who wants to babysit. Obviously you are going to want to know a great deal more about this day-in-day-out person than you had a right to know about the occasional two-hour sitter. You will immediately want to know, for instance, how this person feels about conducting bizarre Satanic rituals on people under five years old. Later you can delve into her personal philosophy on vegetarianism, Bruce Willis movies, and government conspiracy theories.

My friend Julie, who was once interviewing a Pollyannaish young woman who kept going on and on about the joys of little babies and how darling their toes are and how adorable it is when they wrinkle their charming little noses, finally said to the woman: "You are aware, aren't you, that babies cry and spit up and sometimes make grown-ups burst into tears?"

It's best, you see, to have a sitter who suspects what she's in for, and won't later blame you when daily life turns out to be alternately harrowing and boring. By all means, don't conceal the fact that your dishwasher tends to throw sudsy water on the floor every fifth time you use it, and that the baby projectile-vomits whenever she gets reminded of strained carrots, or that you've never once gotten this child to sleep without falling asleep yourself. You don't want to come home one day to find that the sitter left hours earlier without leaving a note.

Warning Signs That Your Sitter Might Not Last

- She has a law degree and she's studying to take the bar exam.
- She says she loves kids because they're so "mellow" and "close to Nature."
- She works nights as an exotic dancer.
- She asks you to buy a motorcycle-safe helmet for the baby.
- When you call home, her boyfriend answers the phone—and says groggily that she's asleep.

The time-honored way to make sure your sitter stays and that she's there for all the right reasons—and doesn't go through your drawers and laugh at your ratty underwear when you're not there—is to fall in love with her and make her your best friend. This does not mean you have to give up your current best friend, the one who chased all the visitors out of your house the day you came home with the baby, and the one who every day reassures you that you do not look like somebody who just gave birth, and that your potbelly is actually adorable on you. You simply have to take on an assistant best friend.

Don't worry. It's not really hard to gain a sitter's devotion. Chocolate bars help, compliments are great, but money really is the key. You have to give her enough money so that when she talks to the other sitters in the park, she doesn't come away thinking she's the lowest-paid human in history. If she thinks that, she just might look the other way when your kid is eating slugs he finds in the sandbox. I hate to say it, but if she's really the vengeful type, she may take samples of your ratty underwear to show around to the other sitters.

Keep in mind that you have to say terrific things to her, too, even though you're tired. For instance, even when you come home and the house is a wreck with toys and the baby is freaking sleeping and it's obvious he'll be up all night because of it, it would be very bad to say, "Boy, you don't know how lucky you are, getting to sit here in my house, watching television, while I have to go out and work for a living." A good rule is never to say anything to her that you would have killed your husband for, had it been said to you back in your stay-at-home days.

Sitters, day-care homes, or centers: What to do?

Many people probably would take more care with their birth control measures if they knew in advance how much trouble it was going to be to find the kid a caregiver. Just having to say the word caregiver out loud can make you break out in hives. It's one of those made-up yuppie words that nobody even heard of until about twenty minutes ago. It hasn't earned its place in the language.

Still, you need one—a caregiver, that is. Many of us don't realize how desperate this search is going to be until approximately an hour before we have to return to work, when we still haven't managed to come up with the right person. We would all do well to learn from my friend Jackie, who, while in the gynecologist's office having been just diagnosed as being three weeks' pregnant, turned to the nurse and said, "So do you know any good caregivers?"

This is the kind of forward-thinking person who can make a go of it in this world without breaking a sweat. I'm sure Jackie had the kid's college picked out by the end of his kindergarten year. For the rest of us, however, even the list of possibilities— short though it is—can be paralyzing. When it comes to child care, unless you were blessed with a self-sacrificing mother, you basically have four options:

- Take the baby and approximately a truckload of paraphernalia and furniture to work with you.
- Hire someone to come to your house.
- Take the baby to a daycare home, where a woman, usually with kids of her own, watches yours and several others.
- Enroll your child in a daycare center.

Of course, there are other, more bizarre child-care arrangements, too—ones in which the mother works an eight-hour shift while the father keeps the kid, and then when she comes home, he leaves for work. This is great if you loathe each other, or prefer writing notes to actually talking, but basically it's a lonely, hardscrabble kind of life, and pretty soon you are likely to discover that you can't remember your spouse's name anymore and you dread his days off because it gets harder and harder to hide the fact that you don't know what to call him.

Here's a look at the good and bad parts of child care to pick from.

Your Child to Work With You

The good part: Your child will always be right there beside you, not being shaken by some exasperated caregiver somewhere. You'll get to see when she learns to walk and hear what her first words are, and you can breastfeed her for years, if you want to—every two hours of your whole long work life. And with the right boss, you can turn your workplace into a Child Palace, complete with toys and cribs and plenty of snacks. She'll befriend your co-workers and get used to having adults around her, and eventually she'll learn to sleep during conferences.

The bad part: Are you kidding?! Do you think you will ever get another thing done in your entire work life with your baby right there, spitting up on your documents and screeching into the telephone? And do you think anyone will ever again take you seriously at work?

The worst part: By the time she's three years old, she'll know everything about your job, and she'll start giving you advice.

Someone to Come to Your House

The good part: You don't ever again have to worry about getting your child ready to go anywhere in the morning. You get yourself ready (much like the old days, except that there will be this little person hiding your shoes and pouring breakfast cereal and milk into your briefcase) and then you get to leave. All that has to happen is the sitter arriving.

If you have a live-in sitter or an au pair, you don't even have to wait for her to arrive. She's already right there, ready to make breakfast for the little one and then take him on a day of adventures and toddler classes.

The bad part: If she's not a live-in sitter, you just know that her car will break down and cause her to be late. She'll need new carburetors, distributors, alternators, tires, and engines—and you'll know every detail of it. She'll get sick. Her boyfriend will get sick. Her sister's kids in Duluth will get sick. There will be no end of the reasons why she can't come in to work that day, or will have to come late.

If she's an au pair, she'll know everything about your whole life: how bad you look in the morning, what you and your husband said to each other last night over dinner when you were both overtired, even how often you change the sheets on the bed. She'll overhear your phone conversations, and you hers. She'll use your best wineglasses to drink RC Cola from, borrow your car on weekends, and invite men you don't know to her room.

The worst part: You will imagine that your husband has fallen in love with her because she's young and energetic, as you used to be, and besides that, she probably doesn't have stretch marks. Her stomach is flat, her breasts probably don't leak, and you will feel mean and suspicious every time you find yourself leaving work at odd hours to come home to "make sure everything's all right."

Home Day Care

The good part: A home day care is a lot like your house, except that the mother who lives there intends to stay home all day and take care of children. Your child will be one of several, which will mean that he learns to share toys, take turns, and figure out how to get an adult to pay attention to him—all of which are social skills he'll need. He'll make friends and get to experience family life all day long, even though you're not there. Sometimes kids pick up useful skills from the daycare mom, like how to sort laundry and dust furniture.

The bad part: Sometimes, let's face it, family life isn't so terrific, particularly other people's. It's bad enough your kid is going to experience all the quirks of your own family, which at least you have a little control over. At somebody else's house, he'll be exposed to lots of other stuff: unemployed husbands, smart-alecky teenagers, afternoon talk shows, ketchup on peanut butter sandwiches.

The worst part: Besides the fact that your child may watch more television than you would like, you also need to consider that sometimes daycare moms think you're a perfectly horrible person for, as they see it, "putting your career ahead of your child's welfare" and going off to work, when anyone can see that a Virtuous Mother would instead stay home and take care of other people's kids.

A Day-Care Center

The good part: At a day-care center, there are several trained, educated staff people at all times, so you won't be left without child care on a moment's notice, and nobody will try to make you feel guilty about bringing your child there. They want you to be able to work. And because there are a lot of staff members, anybody who's feeling frazzled can usually get away from kids for a while—go off and scream somewhere in private, instead of having to try to out-tantrum the toddlers they are taking care of.

Also, at the day-care center, you'll meet other parents who will agree with you that life with kids is both amazing and impossible. You'll feel like a member of that special Parent Club at last, and you can exchange dramatic parenting stories and get reassurance from people whose lives are maybe worse than yours.

Day-care centers also will let your toddler experience the sensual joy of fingerpainting, something that you or a home-based caregiver, being in your right minds, would never consider doing.

The bad part: Sadly, there aren't a lot of good centers available, particularly for infants. Studies show that caregivers are underpaid and overworked, and sometimes—due to the large number of kids—your child may not get the stimulation she needs because other, more vocal or more difficult kids get it all.

The worst part: All babies and toddlers need to have someone who thinks that they are the smartest and cutest and most wonderful kid ever—and certainly Nature's latest entry in the Creating a More Perfect Species contest. Sometimes a kid who goes to day care for eight to ten hours a day isn't as adored by the caregivers there as you might wish.

A good solution for some people is a parent cooperative center, in which parents themselves staff the center for a few hours each week and take turns caring for the children. So what that you're not a caregiver? You can give as much care as the next guy. Also, helping to take care of other people's children with other parents around you teaches you more about parenting than you would learn in a hundred years at home. And the people you work side by side with— changing diapers, serving graham cracker snacks, and rocking toddlers to sleep—will be your friends for life.

Okay, so there's a downside here too. Not only do you have to have a flexible job with a boss who lets you leave for several hours a week, but you've got to remember a basic fact of human nature. Changing diapers and feeding babies is sexy work—unexpectedly so. At the cooperative day care I belonged to, people kept falling in love with each other. It got so commonplace that, in addition to having to hire a part-time janitor, we ended up having an unofficial Day-Care Divorce Lawyer.

Chapter 13: Conversations With a Baby

Early efforts

For a long time you can't get a conversation going with a baby. You have to do all the talking yourself, without much in the way of encouragement. I don't think of myself as a shy person normally, but even I found this disconcerting after a while.

Here's how the typical interchange goes. You and the baby look at each other. You clear your throat and tell the baby how much you love her. You tell her that you have noticed that she has ten fingers and ten toes, and that you think her eyes look like her daddy's, but she seems to have her grandfather's hairline. If you're feeling ambitious, you can tell her the names of all her body parts, including the earlobes and the uvula—parts that many other parents are probably neglecting to mention.

That dispensed with—and no other topics coming to mind— many people will then go off and do the laundry. Maybe, hungering after the sound of a human voice other than their own, they risk brain degeneration by turning on daytime TV talk shows. As we all know too well, though, daytime TV is never a solution. You then have to worry that the words the baby has taken in for the day will include *incest* and *sexual perversity* and *premature ejaculation.*

The trouble with babies, as my friend Ellie once said, is that they don't have much in common with regular people.

Still, you can tell by the fact that they're choosing to stay awake that they want to become one of your kind. All the pediatricians, IQ experts, and college admission counselors stand firm on this point: You've got to keep talking to them.

If you can't think of any subject matter after you've covered your intense affection and the naming of body parts (don't forget the uvula), here's a list of suggestions.

Topics You Might Want to Discuss With an Infant

- What you and the baby are wearing, including any justifications you wish. ("You are looking delightful in your red shirt with a white duck on the front, and I'm still wearing my maternity jeans, although by the time you're in second grade, I hope to give these up once and for all.")
- Your career decisions: whether or not you blew your chances for advancement with that snippy E-mail that ended up in your boss's computer.
- Whether you should have taken Latin in high school.
- Gossip about the neighbors that really, you can't tell another soul.
- Advice you might later forget to give. ("If you need to plug a hole in a wall, a glob of toothpaste should do it. And don't ever buy clothing one size too small on the theory that you'll diet to fit into it.")
- If this were a just world, chocolate would be considered a vegetable. (It does grow, right?)
- Your favorite Beatle and what this says about you.
- Your theory about why Samantha from *Bewitched* didn't simply wrinkle her nose and get a million dollars and save Darren all the trouble of going to work.

Be aware that there are some topics that make babies very upset and that you shouldn't bring up. They don't like

181

anything having to do with the federal income tax code, for instance, or stories of the romantic times you had with your former lovers (this is because babies are very loyal to both parents), nor do they want to hear any upsetting news about the state's highway infrastructure repair. A baby hearing these topics discussed will fuss and scream – and may decide to take up projectile vomiting as a hobby.

Babies also don't like irony, although they appreciate the kind of jokes that have funny noises as part of the punch line. Some babies really go for a spirited debate in which you play both parts, so if you have some unresolved issues in your life, such as whether you should ask for a pay raise after your maternity leave, your baby will be delighted to hear you arguing that out.

So as you can see, even without covering disturbing things, you have a lot to talk about, and by the time you're finishing up these suggested topics, your baby will probably have become something of a talker herself.

At first babies just say, "Aaaaaah, aaaaaah, aaaaaaaaaaah," all the time, and you can tell that they're quite proud of this accomplishment by the way they screw up their little noses and concentrate so hard on it. It's as if they have to consciously direct the signal to the right body part: "Brain: Make that 'aaaah' noise again, and this time lift the elbow and kick the feet. I want to get noticed."

Some kids are perfectly content with this one sound for a long time, feeling that they've done their part toward learning human interaction and now can rest for a while and see what comes of it. Some perfectionist babies won't even go on to the "eeee" sound until they feel they've really got the "aaaah" thing down.

My friend Lisa had a baby who rested so long between sounds that she was just about ready to take him to speech doctors to see why he wasn't moving on to "ooo" and "uhhh." Then one day—Linda swears this is true—the baby shouted out the word peanut. Although I believe Linda

182

utterly and completely, the trouble, of course, was that no one else was in the room at the time to hear it.

For the next six months, everybody who came over to Linda's house would try to make conversation with her baby. We asked him any number of questions: "What is George Washington Carver famous for?" "What kind of farming did Jimmy Carter do?" Even, "What is a charming nickname for babies?"

Nothing.

After a few more months, the kid starting saying the vowel sounds he was supposed to. And when he was about three or so, one day he came into the kitchen where Linda and I were talking and asked for a peanut butter sandwich.

"So you were right," I said to Linda. "He really does say 'peanut.'"

An expose of why they say "Dada" before they say "Mama"

Mothers have been wondering about this forever. There you are, having given this baby valuable real estate right next to your internal organs for nine months, not to mention the fact that you had to stop eating unhealthy foods and switch to foul-tasting yogurt soy wheat bran shakes—and then the kid gets born, and once she's looking around for something to name, the something she picks is "Dada." Nothing about you at all—not even an "mmm," which at least you could take as some kind of nickname for "Mama."

Scientists and speech researchers claim that this is only because "Dada" is an easier word to say than "Mama," and that you shouldn't take it so personally.

But I think we all know what's really going on here. Clearly, guys are getting up in the middle of the night and teaching their babies to say "Dada." They are standing over the crib, whispering, "Dada. Dada. Dada." This also explains why men are so tired, even though you're the one taking care of the baby ninety percent of the time.

Getting babies to call their names is one of the ways they compensate for the fact that they feel jealous that they didn't get to give birth to the kid, and that even now, when the baby's born, they have to go to the kitchen and get a bottle if they want to feed it, while you just open up your shirt. Oh, I know. Guys claim they're not jealous about all that, that they wouldn't even want to have to go through all that pushing and yelling and nursing. But really—even though they cope with the loss as best they're able to—you can just see that they need for that baby to acknowledge them first, that it makes them feel a part of things at last. You have your episiotomy scar; your husband gets the kid flapping his arms and hollering, "Dada!" at the sight of him.

I know. It's not a fair exchange.

I had a kid who not only had a name for Dada, but long before it ever occurred to her that I, too, might have a name, she knew how to say "Kitty" as well. I must admit I pictured the two of them—my husband and the cat, whom he swore he didn't even like—heading into the baby's room together in the middle of the night, whispering, "Dada, Kitty," until morning. But it really didn't bother me that she knew both their names before she knew mine. What was really a slap in the face was that she even had a word for books and newspapers before she considered calling me anything. She'd see any printed material and would start chanting "Bo-bo-bo" in a very determined way. Now what kind of message is that, to have pamphlets spoken of before even the mom?

I'll tell you what it did: It mobilized me to stop telling the baby why Paul McCartney was my favorite Beatle, and how sorry I was not to have taken Latin in high school, and to get down to some important speech lessons. "I'm Mama," I said to her as often as possible. "Ma. Ma. Mmmmm would be an acceptable shortcut, if you're having some difficulty.

I'd like to remind you that I'm the one you shared quarters with for a while. I know my liver got in your way, and I'm sorry about that, but you were pretty tough on my ribs, too, you know. Mama. Mama. Ma. Ma."

It worked, eventually. The day came when she ran into a problem working one of the dials on her busy box, and she screamed out, "Mama!" in a decibel level that could break the dishes in the cabinets.

I wasn't upset. Every baby knows that "Mama" is really a synonym for "Help!"

Baby lingo

Some babies learn to talk but don't want to let their parents know. Maybe they think if they start talking too much, you're going to have them make all your difficult telephone calls—like calling your boss to say you're too sick to work, or phoning the mortgage company to see why they didn't credit your last payment.

My friend Ellie had a baby like that. He didn't speak one word until he was nearly three. Ellie was about to call in the speech therapists and maybe even the National Guard, when he suddenly turned to her one day and said, "I want to watch Mets on TV."

Okay, so he didn't say the *the*. We gave him a little leeway. Ellie herself was so stunned that she turned on the game for him, and during the commercials, I think they discussed whether or not the Mets had a shot at the pennant that year, and his opinion on the expansion teams situation.

It hasn't gone that way with my kids. What happens instead is that they decide to develop their own little private language and then they work on converting the rest of the human race to speaking it. I guess when you're one year old, that seems easier than taking on English, with all its weird grammar rules and inconsistencies.

Still, it didn't work out so well for them. I would attempt to tell them the English word for something, and they would invariably look out into space—much as Adam and Eve probably did when they were naming the animals—and then tell me the real word for the thing.

"Chair," I'd say.

"Ruh."

"Diaper."

"Doe."

"Stroller."

"Tic."

"Encyclopedia Britannica."

"Nnnn."

And that would be that. For quite a long time, I was the only adult in the world who knew that a chair was really a ruh and that a stroller was a tic, and that a single letter of the alphabet would suffice for the entire encyclopedia. Whenever I would use the regular English words, the baby would politely repeat the correct word for my edification. I could see that I was being very carefully and patiently trained in my new language.

There were some rough spots. Once I remember saying, "I think you should abandon this language and figure out how to speak my language. Although you've come up with some interesting words, on the whole, you're going to find more people who talk like me than you."

Eventually I won, of course, but there were times it wasn't clear that English was going to come out ahead as the household language. Some Baby Language words, in fact, we still use. Nobody in the family ever talks about the color yellow without referring to it as "ee-hee-o," which is what one of the kids insisted it be called. And cereal is "cedo" and cookies are, mysteriously enough, called "tukalla."

I got most of the English words accepted, though. That's all I was aiming for.

The word is "no"

The day will come when you have to say "no" to your baby. I know this seems impossible to think about, when you are looking down at a darling little cherub who can't even lick his thumb yet. You've heard enough about parenting to know that you're supposed to "set limits," whatever the hell that means. So far, you feel you've done great at this. You haven't let the kid go anywhere unsupervised, and, for the most part, he's followed your requests to keep all poop and pee in the diaper area.

But the big "no" day will come. Eventually you will have to draw the line with him. Possibly, you think, it will be when he's going to his high school prom, and his wild, undisciplined friends will want him to drive out of state to a hotel room they've rented, and you will have to say, "No, honey, you mustn't go with them. We're having a party for you here at home instead." Or maybe the time will come when you have to say, "No, I don't think it's so terrible if you play basketball and baseball and play the lead in the senior play."

But one day—long before high school—your baby will acquire himself some hand-eye coordination and grab for your earring. It will be clear from the look on his face that he does not intend to let go until he has completely removed your earlobe, if not the entire side of your face.

You will scream, "No!" Believe me, it will surprise even you that you can yell so loud.

After that, you'll see lots of occasions where "No!" is really the only appropriate response. One day he'll locomote over to the stereo—it'll take a while, but he'll get there—and when he does, you can see that he's planning to unload a carton of yogurt inside the CD player. Your career of saying "no" regularly and with great feeling has begun.

But here's the thing about "no": It's one of the easier words to say, and hardly will you have told it to them just even once when they take it for their very own and hurl it at you, along with the strained beets.

"Honey, let's eat some more beets—"

"No!"

"Come on, one more bite—"

"NO!"

"I said, open wide and let the choo-choo train come into the station."

"NO!"

I have found that after children have said "no" three times, they feel justified in throwing whatever it is they are arguing with you about, so if you are having this discussion about strained beets, I think it would be wise to grab the offending beets off the high chair and hightail it out of there before you really have something to scream "no" about.

Be aware, though, that for years to come, they're saying "no" as often as they think they can get away with it. One day it will occur to you that, for every time you've said "no" to your kid, he's said "no" to you a hundred times over. He owns "no."

I swear I heard her say "dammit"

Babies, it must be said, cuss like sailors. One day she's ordering you to change her diaper merely by shouting out, "Doe!"—and then the next day you will be standing in line at the bank, calmly speaking with her about such weighty subjects as the importance of not shredding her cookie all over the bank's nice green carpet, and she will look at you and say loudly, "Dammit, I hate this damn place!"

Nothing prepares you for this. It's as astonishing as if she'd just whipped out the deed to her own apartment, believe me. And yes, although you are shocked into virtual heart failure, you also know that it's hysterically funny. Suddenly nothing has ever been funnier in the whole world. You will want to drop on the ground in laughter, pounding your fists on the floor and wetting your pants. But here's what stops you: the sudden realization that heads all across the bank have swiveled to look at you. And there's not a friendly face in the bunch.

People are looking at you as though it's clear that you and the kid live in the front seat of a 1965 Chevy Nova and get your meals out of restaurant garbage cans, and that you specifically wanted a kid because you thought it would be cute to train her to talk dirty. They may even suspect you're there to rob the bank. You see them pull their own dear pure children protectively toward them. I just hope you're not wearing that T-shirt with the spit-up stains and the big rip under the arm and the "Elvis Lives" logo.

So what do you do when this happens? Probably the best thing ever was what my friend Patty did. She turned to her kid and said, "I do too. Let's get the hell out of here."

Of course, then Patty was too embarrassed ever to go back in that bank, so she had to switch her account elsewhere, which takes up way too much time, especially if you haven't balanced your checkbook in a long time. And who, with a baby, has balanced their checkbook?

No, you need to develop a Public Reaction, I'm afraid. At home, you can ignore it all you want, or beat a hasty retreat so you can laugh about it where the kid can't see. But in public, you have to look just as shocked as everyone else, and furthermore, you have to take Action.

Trust me: It never works with the public to blame the word on someone else—a babysitter, for instance. My friend Suzanne once tried sighing and explaining to the bank patrons that the babysitter she'd hired must have said that awful word around the child, but times being what they are, the public enthusiastically voiced its opinion that if Suzanne wanted a kid so bad, she probably should be home with it twenty-four hours a day instead of hiring stevedores to care for it.

No, that won't do. The public will be very happy if you say in a sweet voice, loud enough for them all to hear, of course: "Now, darling, that is not a nice word, and we don't say that."

You run a very big risk doing this, of course. Your kid already knows that damn is a bad word; that's precisely why she chose it. Chances are, she's going to turn to you and say, just as loudly, "Oh, yes, we do say it. This morning you said to Daddy, 'I hate this damn dump!'"

It does not work, in this circumstance, to get into a debate with your child. Do not say, "Oh, no, I would never say that! You must have misheard me. Mommy would never say such a bad word!" Your child will then only be too happy to tell everyone the fourteen other times she's heard you say such a bad word lately. "... and then when Daddy said he didn't want to change my diaper, you said..."

The public already thinks little enough of you. Cut your losses while you can. Your best bet is to try to keep smiling and looking respectable, and get out of public places as fast as possible.

Talkers of substance: The family secrets unmasked

There is something else you need to know about talking. Small children, who have a lot of time on their hands, tend to be keen observers of what's going on in your life—details they're very happy to share with the world. Even two-year-olds, with their limited vocabulary, can get across plenty of information that your relatives and neighbors are fascinated to hear about.

My favorite was little Kristin, who announced after a trip to the rest room with her mom at a family reunion, "When I get big, I'm going to have a string coming out of my bottom, just like Mommy!"

There is hardly anything you can do at a moment like that, except wish that you had remembered to bring the kid's muzzle along. Believe me, there are going to be lots of times that you wish that.

You'll bring a lot of these incidents on yourself, actually. The thing that always happens is that you'll be having a party and decide that it would be so nice for your child to be a part of things. After all, he's so cute and says such delightful, funny stuff around the house—the way he says "lellow" for yellow, for instance, and how he now says "My love you" instead of "I love you." You really want your friends to see this amazing character at work. So you proudly bring in your sweet little toddler, and he looks around and says, "Mommy, which one is the mean lady?"

The worst is that people believe anything a small child says. Somehow we've gotten saddled with that saying "Out of the mouths of babes," and everyone got convinced that because kids are so much purer than the rest of us, everything they say has got to be true.

But rest assured, even though they do tell on you a fair amount of the time, they also do make stuff up.

My friend Paul was stopped in his tracks when his two-and-a-half-year-old daughter once toddled into a cocktail party he was giving, carrying a drawing she announced was to be called "Daddy in a Tutu." All the parents at the party laughed at how cute this was and would have forgotten about it, except for the fact that the childless people really became quite concerned. There was quite a buzz of whispering after that: Did Paul wear a tutu sometimes, and if so, did he in fact put it on in front of his daughter?

"And what size is it?" said one of the men. "I think we ought to go look for it."

It all got quite complicated and weird, and by the end of the party, I think Paul was wishing he'd invested in some good-quality, off-site child care.

Once you have a child who talks, you can no longer say, "Oh, shit!" under your breath when you mash your finger; you can't exclaim over the number of beer cans in your neighbor's recycling bin; and, above all, you can't tell hilarious stories about the people at work. You have to conduct your life as though television cameras are spying on you—at least until you know for sure the kid is in fourth stage sleep. (Don't make the mistake, as we did, of gossiping right after you put your child to bed. That's when they lie there, bored, straining to hear anything you might be saying that they could later use to get you in trouble.)

They know when they have you, too. One day, as I was dropping my two-and-a-half-year-old at my mother's house for a few hours, he said to his grandmother, "I'm glad I here. Mommy was lelling and lelling last night."

She looked at me. "You were yelling?"

I decided that my best hope here was to pretend that "lell" didn't mean what we all knew it meant and to go off on a wild tangent. "Lulling," I said to my mother. "I was lulling him to sleep."

She kept looking at me.

"He gets that word wrong a lot of times. He says 'lell' but I tell him it's really 'lull.' Lull, sweetheart. I was lulling you to sleep. Didn't I sing you songs and read you a story?"

"Yes. But you lelled too."

I started to try to explain then about the four-hour bedtime ritual, the thirty-five trips up and down the stairs, the requests for water, for juice, for drill bits to sleep with, but my mother put up her hand and said not to bother. I think she remembered that she had lelled quite a bit herself.

Later she told me that the moment in her life when she wished children didn't have vocal cords until they were sixteen was when I was two years old. A delivery man came to the door while she was in the bathroom, so—budding hostess that I was—I went and answered the door. When the guy asked if my mother was home, I beamed at him very proudly and said, "Yes, she's home. But she's making a big poop right now."

The big question of our time: Why?

As if your brain isn't already in overdrive with trying to remember not to gossip about the neighbors and not to go to the bathroom when your child is awake, it will have yet another huge task ahead of it. The dreaded "why" stage comes just about the time kids learn to tell all your secrets.

This is a very famous Kid Stage, and no child has ever wanted to miss it, because it's on their Top Ten Fun Things About Being a Kid.

The way the game is played is this: You say something, anything at all, and the kid gets to ask "Why?" You think up an answer to that, and then you get asked, "Why?" again. The world's record, I think, is forty-seven whys on the topic of eating supper without kicking the high chair leg.

Eventually, of course, you find your way back to the creation of the universe, as in:

"Get on your coat. We're going to the store."

"Why?"

"Because we need to buy some food."

"Why?"

"Because we have to eat."

"Why?"

"Because we want to live."

"Why?"

"Because life is a good thing."

"Why?"

"Because the universe made us that way."

"Why?"

"Because the store closes in ten minutes, so get your coat!"

"Why?"

If you wish, at this point, you can go off on a new trainload of whys—leading to why merchants close at certain hours, why they exist at all, but most likely you will still get back to the equivalent of "Because I said so."

193

The great thing about having a little kid at home is that you get to reexamine your philosophical beliefs all the time. Unlike other people, you'll know exactly what you think about the beginning of time, the existence of God, and the reasons that humans are supposed to wear clothing—because you get to talk about it all the time.

Chapter 14: Parenting in Public

It's not a good idea to yell at little old ladies who offer advice

When you have a baby or toddler with you in public, you will be stunned by how eager strangers are to point out ways you could improve yourself as a parent. They will even take the trouble to cross the street to tell you things you may be doing wrong and to steer you in the right direction. And believe me, you are probably doing most things wrong, from the public's standpoint.

In fact, to hear people tell it, there was once a Golden Age of Babies—and apparently the babies we're putting out today are of an inferior caliber and need to be worked on more thoroughly so they can measure up. People—particularly little old ladies, who were, after all, in charge of the previous babies—will leap over grocery displays just so they can rush over to tell you about the Golden Agers and how superior they were.

Golden Age Babies evidently did everything right: They slept for more than ten minutes at a stretch, they never cried or had tantrums in public, and they worked hard on their baby skills, such as rolling over and playing games of peek-a-boo. I don't think they even spit up, because that would have been ungrateful and wasteful, and babies back then never wanted to be accused of ingratitude.

You can try to explain that the decline in infant quality is not your personal fault, and that you are doing everything in your power to upgrade your baby, but I'm afraid your explanations won't do much good. These types of old ladies see immediately that you and the baby are a hopeless pair; and after giving you a few pointers and some critiques, they will usually dodder off somewhere to buy their milk of magnesia and leave you to your delinquent-raising in peace.

I think you deserve a real treat if you can manage not to yell at them. Not raising your voice to an old lady should earn you at least one can of pink vanilla frosting, which you are allowed to eat in its entirety during the baby's next seven-minute nap. And if you even manage not to sigh and roll your eyes in her direction, then you might also find yourself deserving of a can of whipped cream as well.

I was once in Stop & Shop with my two-year-old, who had decided she couldn't stand living with me anymore because of the way I insisted on hogging the driving each time we went anywhere in the car. To show her displeasure at my selfishness, she kicked at the back of my seat —from her car seat—the entire way to the store. When we got to the parking lot, she lost her mind again because something in the atmosphere reminded her of an amusement park we'd gone to the summer before—and suddenly she wanted to know why Stop & Shop didn't have a roller coaster in the parking lot.

"I want rowwer coasta!" she kept shrieking, interspersed with "Me drive! Me drive to store!"

A wiser person probably would have realized that she really didn't need milk and bread as much as she had earlier thought she did, but I am not that wise, so I went into the store anyway, carrying this kicking and screaming toddler. By then, she'd discovered she was also mad that the Stop & Shop had automatic doors instead of doors she could push open, and also there was a color banner over aisle one that she hated.

Naturally some former Golden Age moms were anxious to help me out. One rushed over almost immediately to assess the situation.

"Your child sounds so unhappy," she said, over the wailing. "Why don't you just this once cuddle her and give her what she wants?"

Now I was raised in the South, where they beat you if you're not unfailingly polite. Being nice to strangers comes very naturally to me, so, although it occurred to me to pick up rolls of paper towels and start throwing them at this woman, I knew I couldn't do it. For one wild moment, I thought of whipping out adoption papers and giving her my daughter to raise. The phrase "If you know so freaking much, you take her!" ran through my head.

Instead, I shifted the kid—who was now in such a back arch that she was practically contorted into a circle—and said to the little old lady very sweetly, "Well, I would, you see, except that what she wants is to have driven the car to the store herself, then to go on a Stop & Shop roller coaster that doesn't exist, and she'd like to have the automatic doors disabled, and for the management to remove that banner."

The lady said, "Oh." Then she looked away. "When my children cried, it was usually because they wanted a cuddle and a little treat."

"Times have changed," I said. "Now they want driver's licenses."

"Well," she said smugly, "back when I had children, we made clear that they couldn't have driver's licenses until they were older. You young mothers need to set your limits."

Fortunately, she left quickly. I had my hand on a lethal roll of paper towels, and I knew just what I hoped to hit with it: her bottle of milk of magnesia.

197

The social stages of babies

Debates with toddlers in the supermarket won't happen to you for quite a while, however. For a long time, you are going to be carrying around a non-talking, adorable little baby, who will keep her roller coaster opinions to herself.

Babies, even before they know how to talk, think of themselves as very social creatures, worthy of being included in everything you do. In this, they resemble dogs, who get offended if they hear the car keys rattle and then see you go off alone into the world. A baby feels there is no social situation that could not be enhanced by having him along.

They do have stages, however. You might as well know now that this is something that everyone will always ask you, now that you're a parent: "What stage is he in?" They ask this question as though all you have to do is consult your handy Baby Reference Guide, check off his accomplishments and/or symptoms, and then rattle off the name of some developmental stage.

Of course babies are always going in and out of stages, mixing everyone up. To answer correctly, you'd have to say something like, "Well, he's in the food-hurling, stranger-adoring, no-sleep-ever stage," which would make everyone give you odd looks and possibly leave you alone after that. To ensure that you're never asked this question again, you could even call up the questioner in a few days and report that you sense the "car seat-resisting stage" is just about to begin, and perhaps later in the week you'll hope for the "nap-for-ten-minutes" stage. You could promise to give hourly stage updates.

But if you really want to pull out something that sounds official, here are some possible Social Stages of Babies.

The Blob Stage: This is obviously in the early days, when you are allowed to lug the baby around as though she were a pillow from the sofa instead of anything lifelike. She won't know or care where she is as long as certain basic requirements are met: plenty of food, something to throw up on, and no sunlight shining in the eyes. (Babies think that the sunlight is a special infant torturing device, and they will flip out, flailing their arms and legs and screwing up their little faces if you let the sun hit them.)

Socially, babies in the Blob Stage are a mess, although this doesn't stop them from being pretty popular with others. They make faces, fall asleep, yawn in front of company, and often let loose with bodily function noises. Adult conversations bore them utterly, and they make no pretense of having an okay time if conditions aren't to their liking.

The Flirt Stage: Along about three months of age, babies see that they themselves are indispensable in social situations. They feel ready to take over your social life for you, jumping in to flirt with your friends and even hailing passersby in the hopes of starting up relationships quite independent of you.

Once I was having a row with the manager of a department store, who seemed to think I shouldn't mind that my credit card had been billed twice for the same infant sweater—and the whole time I was making my points, punctuating with my finger in the air, I noticed the manager trying to keep from laughing. The man could not seem to keep his composure. Finally, I looked over at my six-month-old baby, riding on my hip. She was grinning at him and making funny faces and shaking her finger in the air in a perfect imitation of me.

Obviously this was an act of treason, but who could get mad? In that case, she may have helped get us some satisfaction, since he did finally fix the bill. Worse is when you turn around to see that they've taken up with motorcycle gang members and Colombian drug lords, and have somehow indicated— with their winning smiles and flashing eyes—

that they, too, would like to have their entire bodies tattooed with pictures of cobras.

Once a man, so tattooed he looked like the comic page of the newspaper, announced to me that my eight-month-old son was enamored of tattoos and that I really ought to take down the number of a tattoo parlor and keep it for future reference.

"He's a bit young," I said. "I don't think he knows what he'd be getting into."

"Naw, not now," said the guy, who, in addition to plenty of reptile tattoos, also sported plenty of black leather and chains and even some delightful beer breath. "Even I didn't get my first tattoo until I was ten! Whaddya think, I'd tattoo a baby? All's I'm saying is he's interested. Now take Vinnie the Snake's card—"

He thoughtfully left out the phrase we both knew was elliptical: "before I kill you."

We looked down at my child, who by now was holding out his arms, practically begging Mr. Tattoo Breath to take him away and raise him in the motorcycle tattoo parlor where live snakes no doubt crawled around on the floor with the babies.

"Lookit how much he likes me!" crowed the guy.

Later I decided it was simply because they had the same number of teeth.

The Shrinking Violet Stage: Then, for no good reason and without warning, your child will one day decide that she's made a dreadful mistake in consorting so blithely with the human race at large. From now on, she intends to screech in abject terror whenever anyone enters her imaginary personal space, which on some days will seem to be four miles in diameter. She will cower when little old ladies try to stroke her cheek, stiffen in fear when your mother approaches, and cling to you for dear life when she figures out that you're leaving her with a babysitter.

You will feel as if you're raising a psychopath, the kind who will move to wilderness Alaska at age sixteen and live on bugs and tree bark and write manifestoes calling for the end of human civilization.

Most people aren't very helpful when you're going through this stage with your baby either. "Ewww," they'll say. "Certainly not a very friendly baby you've got there," as though you're secretly telling him bad things about humans when you're alone together. But don't worry. Like other stages, this one will also pass.

The Jerry Lewis Stage: Once babies really get it that you're not seeking to beat a hasty permanent retreat and that most human beings are really okay once you get to know them, they take on a new calling. They decide that their function as Little People in the World is to regale the rest of us with their wit and charm. Even if they can't talk yet, they're always ready with some slapstick humor, designed strictly for the purpose of showing you a good time.

Babies really go in for that pie-in-the-face kind of stuff, just as soon as they can manage it. This is one reason you might want to keep cream pies away from your child, in case you were thinking otherwise. Although it must be said that an eight-month-old, even without a cream pie at his disposal, is perfectly capable of amusing everyone in his vicinity with loud raspberries, particularly the kind that propel some sort of food device outward onto the face of an onlooker. This is the stuff of high humor to a baby comedian.

As time goes on, they polish their material to a fine sheen. You will see them making funny faces, squirting food out of their nose, and doing fan dances with their bath towels, all strictly for laughs. You may not want to be raising the next Jerry Lewis, but it's a stage you have to endure just the same.

Of course there are plenty of other substages that pop up here and there: the Chimpanzee Stage, when it would really be helpful to take them around on a leash; the Biting

Stage, when a muzzle is just the thing but looks so tacky on a human child; the Bull in the China Shop Stage; the Sarah Bernhardt Stage; the Dismantler Stage; and on and on.

Nature's little joke

If you've ever wanted proof that Nature has a sense of humor, you get it when your baby learns to walk. Here is this momentous milestone of development that you've been waiting for— and then it turns out that Nature gives kids the ability to walk about six months before it gives them their full set of brains.

The only explanation I can come up with is that Nature has a primitive, slapstick sense of humor, and that the sight of little people hurtling about is thought to be comical.

Well, it probably is funny, except when you're the person who has to save your baby's life thirty times a day. I think it would have been just a bit more humane to hold off giving children walking skills until certain key components— like fear, caution, and the ability to slow down—had been installed in the program.

Babies get upright, take their first steps, and then within minutes are chasing the ice cream truck down the street.

There's about a three-month period where all you do is run after them, steering them out of the paths of oncoming Mack trucks, grabbing hold of their shirts as they are about to plummet down a set of stairs, and throwing your body between them and concrete walls. They run full blast into poles, careen into tables and chairs, and hurl themselves through rosebushes. They get up and keep going, of course, since they're built low to the ground. You are left gasping for breath, and shaking from excess adrenaline.

The trouble is the public. Sometimes you will see people glaring at you, as though when you were placing your order for a child, you insisted that you get one with lots of

202

speed and very little sense. Jeanne, a friend of mine, once rescued her eleven- month-old walker from about seventeen different bashing accidents, and turned her face to the sky, and shouted, "Please! Please hook up the brains!" But the public was not amused.

The catalog companies could be helping out here. If they can't manage to supply temporary brains you could insert until your own child's have grown in properly, then the least they could do is invent some kind of rubber suit-and-helmet outfit so your baby can be fully protected from bumps—along with a sonar tracking device for you. And maybe an IV sedative drip for the two of you.

Babies out to eat

I have to tell you what happens when you try to take a baby or small child into a restaurant: You will see people actually get up out of their assigned seats and beg the waiter to let them sit somewhere else, anywhere else. It's a whole social phenomenon. I have seen grown-ups pleading with head waiters and shelling out wads of dollars so they could even get a table next to the Dumpster rather than endure what they imagine your little one is going to put them through.

They are probably smart to do this, of course. At least when you're sitting next to the Dumpster, you know what to expect: the smell of rotting food, the possible appearance of small rodents. But with a small child, anything at all could be awaiting you.

Once, in a Japanese restaurant, a couple a few tables away from us apparently tired of listening to their toddler's screams from the high chair and so released him to the restaurant at large. (This is a felony in some states, I believe.) His mission, it turned out, was to bring sushi to each table and calmly deposit it on people's shoes, while saying, "Shoesi, sushi." Although I, as a parent, admired the delicate subtlety of such a joke, others seemed horrified to find themselves wearing raw yellow-tailed tuna on their feet.

What people without children don't know is that we, the parents, don't like this any better than they do. You think those people wanted their kid to wander around the restaurant decorating footwear with pieces of raw fish? You can bet they did not. But the alternative—eating at home—was to them so hideous, so unthinkable, that they simply had to get out into the world with their child, and if that meant heading into a restaurant and being given hostile looks by waiters and customers alike—well, then that's just the price they had to pay.

Why, you may ask, was eating at home so hideous and unthinkable?

This we can't really say, of course. In my case, it's often been because the only things we had at home to eat were a jar of lemon zest and a cucumber, and it was too damned much trouble to start at the beginning again, acquiring groceries from a store and then having to cook them. The choice was either to find a restaurant and take the kid into it with us or to face starvation.

Then there are those times when you think, "What the hell? I want to eat out, and by God, I'm taking the kid!" This is known in psychiatric circles as denial.

One year we went on vacation to Montreal with our eleven-month-old daughter along. Because we were taking the train, we didn't feel able to bring our normal load of furniture and baby paraphernalia along on the trip. Amtrak really wouldn't hear of our bringing along our full-size high chair, for one thing. And so it happened that one night we really wanted to go to a wonderful French restaurant we remembered from our courtship there.

Obviously we had to take the baby with us. There was no one to babysit, and we were completely, selfishly unwilling not to go to this restaurant that had once meant so much. No one could have reasoned with us, I'm afraid. We were deeply in denial, believing that anything was possible.

First, we called the restaurant to see if they even allowed babies. After a brief muffled consultation, it turned out that they did. And did they have a high chair? Another muffled conversation, then yes. We did high fives in the air.

When we got there it turned out what Montrealers thought of as a high chair was just that: a wooden bench set high off the ground. You couldn't put an eleven-month-old on it and expect her to stay there. She was just entering the chimpanzee substage, when she really needed to be tied up through most of her waking hours. We sat miserably through the first part of a candlelit evening, passing our restless daughter back and forth across the table between us and taking turns eating. After she had kicked at a table leg so hard the whole table almost fell down, thrown wads of French bread into the air, and rubbed butter into the tablecloth, she then busied herself with standing in my lap, facing the wall. I was puzzled by how absorbed she seemed to be with this position but was managing to eat with my left hand and grip onto her with my right, when my husband said, "Uh, honey, she's taking the painting off the wall."

Later we had a not-very-romantic dinner in our hotel room, watching Canadians speak French on TV, while we passed the doggie bag back and forth.

But, bad as that is, it's worse once they learn to talk. Then they feel compelled to talk to people at the other tables, and talk loudly about the people at the other tables.

"What that yucky thing that man eating?" is a common restaurant question, and take my advice and try to come up with an answer quickly, or there will be guesses. Once, the man at the next table happened to be enjoying some link sausages, which grossed out our twenty-month-old. "Look!" she shrieked. "That man eating cat poops! Tell him no, Mommy."

Besides their commentary on other people's menu selections, they also want to stand up in their high chairs—obviously so they can have a wider audience to appreciate them. They shout out their baby jokes, clapping their hands and rubbing food into their hair—always big hits at home, and even try to enlist calm, well-behaved children into their little comedy show. I once kept urging my daughter to sit down until finally she glared at me and yelled out, "You, killjoy!"

But if you lose your mind temporarily and happen to find yourself in a restaurant with a toddler, do not, under any circumstances, go to the rest room. Wet your pants if you have to, but don't go anywhere near the bathroom. Babies are famous for their desire to share information with others, and if you leave them at the table, they are sure to stand up on the chair and announce to everyone where you've gone and speculate about what you might be doing in there. My friend Elbe's kid yelled out, "I think my mommy has a big tummyache!"

And if you take them along to the rest room with you, they will report to the restaurant clientele just what transpired as soon as the two of you come back out.

"Mommy went pee, but the potty was too misgusting for me." Toddlers, most of whom snack on dryer lint and like to rub sandbox dirt into their nostrils, often are of the opinion that public toilets are too filthy for their delicate selves to bear—a fact you may not wish to have broadcast at large to the other diners.

After a few trips to a restaurant with a toddler, the concept of take-out food will start to make a lot of sense to you.

The fine print on the baby contract
There are some restaurant success stories, however. My friends Linda and Bill have been taking their two-year-

old out to dinner with them for months. In fact, Linda didn't even know you could get take-out food, that's how successful these ventures had been. One night I ran into them in a restaurant—okay, so I was spying on them—and sure enough, little Max was sitting in his high chair, nibbling on some crackers, and Linda and Bill were talking quietly while they ate dessert. Dessert! A totally luxurious part of the meal. Linda, I observed, wasn't even eating at the speed of ninety miles per hour, which is the way that I thought all mothers of small children were required to eat.

I knew there had to be some horrible little secret as to how they got this to happen. I almost thought I should call the authorities and have Max tested for drugs. But then Linda told me that no, it wasn't pharmaceutical at all. They had simply had Max sign a contract.

Did I mention that Max is two?

Maybe it's only because both Linda and Bill are corporate attorneys and they know how to get somebody to sign a contract, but they had actually convinced their son that if he didn't sign an agreement to behave in a restaurant, he would get left at home with a sitter. He signed. And then, Linda said, whenever he would get restless and start asking to get a piggyback ride on the waitress or to have the water glasses poured on the other diners, Linda would simply take his contract out of her purse and flourish it in front of him.

"See this, Max? This is your signature." (It looked more like a scribble, but she said that Max had a very sophisticated signature—like a lot of important people do, actually.) "This means that you've given your word that you would sit quietly and let Mommy and Daddy finish the meal."

Naturally I wanted a copy of that contract. It said:

"I promise to be a good boy in the restaurant and not to get out of my high chair, cry, or otherwise disturb the other diners. I will not ask to leave until Mommy and Daddy have both finished their meals. Signed, Max."

Obviously this was an airtight deal, and it was working.

I started thinking of all the things I'd get my kids to sign: contracts for bedtime, sleeping through the night, eating spinach without throwing it, not begging for things at the store, agreeing to ride in the car seat without screaming. We could have legally binding contracts all over the house.

But Linda told me she didn't think that would really be wise. "You only get to pick a couple of things that are serious enough for a contract," she said. "Otherwise they just go on strike, and then you've got those horrible binding arbitration hearings to go through. And judges, as you might predict, always sympathize with the little guy."

Kids and manners: "Congratulations for having me over"

You might think, from hearing the warnings about small children in public, that they are mostly wild savages not to be tolerated by most civilized beings. This is, of course, true. But the day does come when they want to be part of civil discourse. They notice, for instance, that you and your friends hardly ever throw food at each other or wad up pieces of bread before stuffing them into your mouths.

They want manners, too. My friend Lillian had a daughter who once, very adorably, served water in paper cups to a lot of women who were over for a visit. It was only later that Lillian realized where it had come from, when she saw her daughter toddle over to the toilet to scoop out a cup of water to drink for herself.

But hey, it's the thought that counts. Babies' generosity is truly a wonderful thing to watch. You spend months feeding them their baby food, or trying to, and then one day they pick up a banana and decide to feed it to you. You can't miss that determined look in the eye, and the sound they make of the choo-choo train going into the station, as the banana makes its way toward you. Take my advice and open wide, or else you're going to have a nostril full of mushy fruit.

They also pick up fairly quickly on the fact that there are socially acceptable words that have to be said: *please* and *thank you* and *I'm sorry*, for instance. I'm sure that, to their ears, the whole world sounds like: "Okay, now, Peter, say please to the nice lady. Okay, now say thank you. Oops, Peter, you dropped it. Say I'm sorry, and then say please for another one. Okay, now say thank you. And say again that you're sorry—"

If it weren't well documented that most little kids are already a bit on the crazy side, you could see that hearing this all day might tend to make them go a little nuts. After all, it's tough to keep all this straight. I used to have to rehearse with one of my children: "No, no, it's please when you want something, and then thank you when you get it. Sorry isn't until it's all gone wrong."

We just about had this all down right, too, and then a friend of mine announced she was getting married. "Congratulations!" I said to her. And then later, "Congratulations" to the bridegroom and to the bride's mother who, frankly, didn't think these two were ever going to get married.

A few days later we were visiting some friends, and when it came time to go home, we were all exchanging pleasantries and thanks for the lovely evening, that sort of thing. I saw my two- year-old's face distorted with deep thinking. It was clear he was trying to come up with just the right thing to say.

When it was his turn to say goodnight, he burst out with, "'Gratulations for having me over."

My friend didn't even blink. She said, "Well, 'gratulations to you for coming to my house."

After that, we used congratulations interchangeably with thank you, as in "Congratulations for picking up your socks" and "Congratulations for not running me down with your tricycle." Later, much later, it even became a loose substitute for "I'm sorry," as in: "Congratulations for not killing me when I spilled grape juice into your CD collection."

Can you say "incentives"?

Many people will tell you that it's bad to start a bribery system with small children, but I say how the hell else are you going to take them out in public? It's either bribe them or scream at them, the way I see it, and I'm sorry, but bribery is something you can accomplish without other people knowing about it, whereas with screaming, most everyone will find out.

Bribery is what oils the machinery of interaction between parents and children, especially in public, where you really might prefer to go about your business without having police officers interfering.

You just have to develop a good way of doing it, that's all. For instance, it never works, when bribing a child, to relinquish the power role by whining at them. We've all heard mothers in public who long ago lost the upper hand and are reduced to whimpering blobs: "Pleeeease, Justin honey, sit in the cart for Mommy, and I'll buy you anything you want—a new house, a Jaguar, an airplane hangar."

There are several things wrong with this scenario. First of all, little Justin by this point is behaving so badly that the entire population of the grocery store would rather see him spend the rest of the shopping trip in the meat locker. The store manager, in fact, would gladly escort him there and close the door. Obviously this mom missed the moment for bribery, which always has to be long before the child's behavior is so horrible that the criminal justice system is interested in taking his name.

Bribes have to be offered when you're still in the position of strength. And it's important to know just what to offer. Justin's mother may have wanted a new house, a jaguar, and an airplane hangar, but Justin could more easily be bought off by a seedless grape.

I once heard a woman in the doctor's office promise her kid a pony if he would stop tapping on the window blinds. Obviously this was a flagrant violation of the Rules of Bribes, and several of the other mothers glared at her. Later one woman took her outside and said, "The going rate for a kid not tapping on window blinds is one green M&M. Not even a red one. And here you are, promising a pony? What are you going to pay for him getting into his car seat without shrieking—a full home zoo and tickets to a Barney marathon?"

The pony woman apologized profusely and said she hadn't known there was a currency rate for bribes.

Oh, but there is. Mostly M&Ms are the currency of choice, although I have heard that there are very strict parents out there who can get babies to work for raisins, and a woman in Cleveland who got her children to do anything she wanted by promising them extra bedtime stories. These are extreme cases, however, probably worthy of being written up in books about parenthood anomalies. For the most part, you've got to come across with little colored pieces of candy if you want things to go smoothly in the world, and it helps if you know what the different colors are good for. There's no excuse for squandering a red or a yellow on something you know you could have gotten with a green. And nothing is worth a pony—unless it's a lifetime of sleeping through the night, sitting quietly in the high chair, and never once asking for anything in a store.

Current Bribery Rates for Toddlers

Getting into the car seat without screaming
2 orange
Sitting down in the grocery store cart
1 green
Not removing diaper in public
1 blue
Not smearing fingers on the wall of the bank
1 red
Not biting anyone in the sandbox at the park
2 yellows
Removing mittens on the hottest day of the year
3 reds
Not screaming during hair-washing ordeal
4 blues and a red
Agreeing to use the potty chair
Whole bag

One more tiny little warning: There may be people you don't want to use the word bribe around. It does have such an undeservedly negative connotation. I've found that for some, it's important to think of these as "incentives."

Call it what you will—it works.

Chapter 15: Life in the Terrible Twos

What means whining?

One of the favorite pastimes of people in America today is to tell you how much you're going to suffer when your adorable newborn gets to be two years old. I think, in many social circles, warning people about the Terrible Twos is even bigger than antiquing.

Now you're starting to panic, thinking maybe they're right about two-year-olds.

But here's what they neglect to mention: Living with a two-year-old is fascinating. Two-year-olds have strong opinions. They have deep thoughts. They also make excellent dictators.

There's something almost humbling about giving birth to a tiny blob of human protoplasm, and then watching in amazement as it gradually develops a way of life for itself, each day taking on more and more people-like qualities—and then one afternoon, quite out of the blue, it orders you to push a rubber band around in the doll stroller for the rest of the day.

You do wonder how it is that your life got to this point. But here's the weird thing: You don't object. You're too flabbergasted. It's as dumbfounding an experience as if your house cats had suddenly asked you to take them for a drive, and wondered would you mind if they smoked in the car.

It takes a while for that amazement to wear off, and until it does, you're going to find yourself doing all sorts of two-year-old-pleasing activities, things that in a million years you wouldn't have been able to think up. You will realize that there's no one else in the world you would do this for. But not only will you take rubber bands for stroller rides, but you'll also wear socks on your ears, eat pretend mud cakes, and force-feed bananas to baby dolls. There will be days that you just pray no adult is going to ask you what you did during the last twenty-four hours; it's hard to admit that you gave an onion a bath and then put an undershirt on the cat. Some nights you get into bed and the only thing you can point to that you've done right all day is that you didn't let your two-year-old play on the highway, no matter how loudly she screamed at you.

But as fun and inventive as all this is, there is something about toddlers that I feel I must warn you about. They whine. Somehow, programmed into their DNA is information about the exact pitch of noise that you—with your particular form of related DNA—cannot bear. I think Nature designed it that way on purpose. Other kids can whine all they want, and you won't even care. But let yours start up, and all the hairs will stand up on the back of your neck, your blood supply will start bypassing valuable areas in your brain, and your limbs will freeze.

Kids know this about the sound of whining, too. They are well aware that they possess a noise that is so excruciating that it shuts down some neurological connections in most adults, particularly their parents. It is a weapon that was given to them at birth, somehow meant to help ensure their survival, but as with all weapons, sometimes it just causes escalation of the difficulties. I have seen parents succumb to their paralyzed stupors and collapse, writhing in agony on the ground—and with no soundproof booth and cold drink around to save their lives. Now where does that get a child?

Even though children know they have this power, they're not precisely sure what you're talking about when you tell them not to whine—how it differs, say, from the other annoying things they do like crying and falling on the ground in a rage. After telling my two-year-old to "Stop whining!" about fifteen thousand times over the course of her life, she once stopped dead in her tracks and gave me a blank stare.

Then she said, "What means whining anyway?"

I said, "It's that half-crying, half-talking thing you do that makes my hair turn green and my face sprout boils, and sends me crashing to the floor in a horrible heap. That is what means whining."

She said, "Oh."

It had been the first intelligent conversation we'd had on the subject.

Okay to bread boats, but here are twenty-one things I did refuse to do in one afternoon

A day will come when you find yourself home alone with a cranky toddler. No matter how carefully you have planned your life, how much your mother and mother-in-law want to be keeping her, how many consecutive out-of-town jobs you have secured for yourself, there will come a day when you have no way out.

It is raining outside. Your child is whining, making that noise. You happen to notice that your household owns no arsenic.

And then your toddler says that you are to wear some bread boats.

"Bread boats," she says ominously, sounding like Marlon Brando in *The Godfather,* "bread boats wanna go for a ride."

If you do not right now have a two-year-old to instruct you, you might not know that bread boats are torn-up pieces of bread, buttered on at least one side, that will be affixed to you so that you can take them for a ride. Your job is to walk around and around the dining room table until they've had enough. And how long until a piece of bread has had enough riding around a table is a question that has perplexed philosophers for centuries. The answer, I think, is as close to infinity as you're going to find these days.

Okay, so I have done this. I did it for as long as I could stand it, which was up until I noticed that the dining room shades were open and that my neighbors were home. I could just picture them nudging each other and her saying, "Look over now, Carl. That child has her wearing little pieces of toast!"

Some people would think that this might have been wimpy of me. They would say that I should have drawn my line and insisted, with all my rightful authority as a parent, that this was not going to happen.

What you don't realize unless you're the parent of someone of this age and potency is that you are forever drawing your line and threatening with the full force of your parental authority. That same afternoon of the bread boats, I had exerted my authority on twenty-one other things. I even ended up going back into the kitchen and reapplying the butter when the damn things kept falling off—and, after closing the shades, I wore them for a few more dozen trips around the table before I suggested we might eat them as a snack—an idea that was rejected immediately.

But here's the stuff I didn't do:

- I said she couldn't take her nap outside, even if she wore her raincoat.
- I wouldn't let her sleep with the Elmer's glue, the black marking pens, the yardstick, and a dinner fork.
- I said no disposable diaper on the cat.
- I refused to take the car keys out of the ignition so she could play with them while I was driving.
- I said we couldn't wear the cat's dishes on our heads.

- I would not take the vacuum cleaner outside to suck up all the ants.
- I said that more than twenty Band-Aids on a person with no injuries was excessive and wouldn't be tolerated.
- I said she couldn't wear Daddy's shoes when we went to the store.
- I didn't let her eat butter right out of the tub.
- I didn't let her pour the box of corn flakes into the bathtub while the water was running.
- I refused to try to regurgitate a piece of apple I had just eaten, which had just been found to be The Most Wonderful Piece of Apple Ever to Exist in the World.
- I didn't let her throw the desk lamp down the laundry chute.
- I was extremely firm about not allowing the wading pool to come in the kitchen so we could both swim while I cooked dinner.
- I said we couldn't paint our faces with the strawberry yogurt.
- I said no to licking the rain-soaked rocks on the front porch.
- I said we couldn't put the goldfish and the cat together on the floor to see who would win in a fight.
- I refused to let her ride her tricycle down the cement steps.
- I said she couldn't cut her own bangs.
- I said I couldn't staple the bread boats to myself, that it was butter or nothing.
- I said we couldn't dump out the soy sauce and drink our apple juice in the soy sauce bottle.
- I wouldn't let her push me in the doll stroller.

You can see that compared to all this, wearing a few pieces of bread is practically nothing. Besides, it was a crunchy whole wheat bread, and every now and then, I got to eat a piece surreptitiously. Far worse than putting up with the bread boats was when I happened to ask the inflammatory question: "Would you like a piece of cheese?"

I don't know why that was The Question from Hell, but I have learned that when a person crashes to the floor, screaming and kicking and calling for the powers of darkness to destroy me, I have asked the wrong question. I accept this.

Never do anything once you're not willing to do a billion times

I once did a ridiculous thing. I gave my two-year-old a bath while I was wearing a hat with a whirligig on the top. This is obviously something that no thinking person would ever do, and I can only explain it by saying that I had just endured an incredibly difficult afternoon entertaining out-of-town guests (the childless, judgmental variety) and that my brain wasn't operating under full power—or even its usual one-quarter power. I was exhausted and I had a headache, and for some reason, it seemed that a funny hat might just that once expedite the bath process. You know, distract the baby from the fact that she was undergoing the soap and water treatment.

If you are thinking of wearing a whirligig hat in front of a toddler, let me just tell you: Be careful. Wear it once, and you'll be forced to wear it a lot. In my case, it became known as the Bath Hat, and every night for the next eight months I was made to wear it again. We couldn't have bath time without the Bath Hat, which often meant tracking it down in whatever corner of the house it was currently hiding and uncrimping it so it could be jammed onto my head. I was just glad this happened during the time our camera happened to be broken, so there are no permanent records of this.

You will notice that rituals come from parental desperation. Therefore, it's best if you can somehow avoid that all-over panicky feeling that you'll do anything to get your child moved along to the next step of the day. Sometimes you won't be able to do this unless you have taken thirty years of yoga classes and also possess the ability to walk on hot coals. But if you only take on, say, three new rituals a day during the year that your child is two, then I think you have made excellent progress.

Another one that I got myself into by accident happened during the morning drop-off at day care. One morning my child was whining and clinging to me when it was time to say goodbye, and in a panic, I said, "Would it help if you rubbed my elbow three times before I leave?"

I don't know what prompted me to think of this as a rare prize, but his face lit up and I knew I'd hit on something big. Naturally, though, for the next two years, we could never part without him calling pitifully after me, "I need three of elbow!" During particularly stressful times, he would request "five of elbow" and "ten of elbow," and on one memorable trip to the testing center for kindergartners, "a hundred of elbow."

Let me tell you, there is hardly more ridicule and scorn you can ask to have heaped on yourself than if you get involved in an elbow-stroking deal with your child. My friends were hysterical over this. "I can just see him when he's old enough to date," my friend Patty said. "He'll be out at the drive-in with some girl and begging her to let him fondle her elbow. He's going to be quite a hit with the ladies."

Goodbye rituals are particularly dangerous. The child knows you have to get away, and that he holds the key to your departure. He can make it take a very long time or a very, very long time. All power is in his hands, and you will do anything—tap dance, sing a ridiculous song, make up a new little poem—just so you can leave with him smiling at you as you go.

Do not make up a little poem. In fact, do not do anything that you wouldn't gladly do every single day for the rest of your life with this child, or you will be intensely, dreadfully sorry.

It's important to get yourself a ritual that you are happy to live with. "I know what," you can say. "We'll have a deal where every morning when we say goodbye, I'll count to three and dash for the car, and you'll smile and wave bye-bye."

Falling out of favor

It doesn't matter how many bread boats you have worn, how many baths you've willingly done with whirligig hats, how many three-of-elbows you have given, the day comes when your child wants nothing to do with you. The sun that used to rise and sit on your head has set. You are not fit to pour the next glass of juice.

To make matters worse, it's that other parent who's now glorified and adored. Only he is wonderful enough to be allowed to remove a child from the crib, or to change a poopy diaper, or even read *Goodnight, Moon* 548 times. Sorry. Your contract is up, and it looks as though it won't be renewed.

You can't believe it, but you're devastated by this. It's like seventh grade all over again, only without the note passing. You find yourself wanting to point out all you've ever done for the kid, starting with the prenatal vitamins you remembered to take every day, and all the oxygen you politely sent down the umbilical cord. Never mind the months of stroller rides, the goodnight rituals you've faithfully followed, and even the fevers you've worried over. But then you remember that this is a toddler, for God's sake. They don't subscribe to the favor system that the rest of the earthlings know.

Once I foolishly poured apple juice in the wrong Tom & Jerry glass. I used a glass with a picture of them flying a kite painted around its middle. The last time I had checked, it had been the favorite glass, but evidently during the night, it had somehow become the most despicable, disgusting glass that a child could ever come in contact with, and there I had stupidly poured a glass of juice in it, without permission.

My daughter drank the juice anyway, without even saying anything, but later I realized she had stopped talking to me.

"What's the matter?" I asked her.

No answer.

"Why don't you talk?"

No answer.

A few minutes later I heard her telling her father that she wanted some juice.

"But I just gave you some juice," I said.

She wouldn't even look in my direction. "She gave me juice in a yucky glass," she told him. "I hate the Tom and Jerry kite glass!"

He was so wonderful that he poured the juice into a more acceptable container, shaking his head and saying, "Sometimes Mommy just doesn't get it. I've never liked the idea of Tom and Jerry flying a kite either. Too dangerous."

After he left for work, I pulled her aside and said, "I think you ought to know that when you're sixteen, I'm the one who's probably going to see that you get a car—while he is going to insist that you pay the insurance yourself. Also, just so you know, he doesn't think girls should date or wear makeup until they're in college."

I'm not ashamed to admit that, in addition to imparting damaging information, I've also tried bribery in the toughest of these cases. I've promised incentives like putting jelly on the zwieback and being willing to overlook the afternoon nap, thinking that might bring me back into favor. I've even pledged to do extra stroller walks and to sing all the verses of "The Wheels on the Bus," including every toddler's favorite, the one where the manifold clunks.

But then one day it hit me what I was doing. Not to be in favor is actually a valuable gift. It's a time of liberation.

When you're not in favor, you get to eat your own dinner without anybody climbing on you and asking for bites of your mashed potatoes. You get to skip the bath and even the long, drawn-out bedtime ritual. You don't have to read the story about P. J. Funnybunny and his quest to see if life as another animal would be good for him.

Do you know what you do when you're not in favor? You go into the kitchen and pour a glass of wine and then you call up a friend of yours (a childless friend, unless you know somebody else who's also not in favor with her kid) and you chat. If you want, you can go and take a long, hot bath yourself—with bubbles and a book—and do your nails. You make sure to remember to use the Tom & Jerry kite glass the next day, too. And the day after that and the day after that and the day after that.

Just don't make the mistake of trying to leave the house at a time when you're not in favor: There's nothing like the idea of you leaving home to bring your status right back up to number one.

Toddler Lit 101

I've heard people say that surely one of the best parts about having children must be that you get to relive all the great moments of your own childhood—the splendid books your parents read to you, the wonderful games you played with your pals, even your favorite movies and television shows.

All I can say is, Ha!

Anyone who's had a kid could tell you that's not how it goes at all. Oh, you may go out and buy the complete collection of A. A. Milne, in the hopes of smiling with your child over the delightful subtleties of Winnie-the-Pooh, but that is never going to happen. Instead, your toddler is going to glom on to some book in which the main character is a turkey named Edna who gets mad because her tail feathers

222

aren't as pretty as the ones belonging to a turkey named Elbert. Then she discovers that Elbert is really a duck, or some such thing, and she decides that to live life to the fullest, she will have to learn to appreciate herself for the turkey she is.

"And then," I always wanted to add, "the farmer came along and made Thanksgiving dinner out of Edna because she was such a twerp."

You get finished with a book like this, and even before your mouth has finished squeezing off the last word, your child is saying, "Again. Read again."

So you read it again, this time only barely able to keep from graphically describing the scene where Edna is served at the farmer's table.

"Again. Read again."

With your last two brain cells, you muster the strength for one more time.

"Again."

"Let's read something else," you say. "How about the story of when Pooh got the honey jar stuck on his nose?"

"No. Edna."

You read the goddamned story of Edna one more time. This time, just to keep yourself conscious through it, you decide you're not going to say any of the thes. It will be a challenge to see if your brain can remember to do this through the entire twenty-six-page tome.

But as soon as you skip the very first the, your kid is right on top of it.

"The," she says.

"What?"

"The, Mommy. It says *the* barn." As if you're not very bright.

You don't want to tell your own dear child the truth, which is that if you have to read the story of Edna and include all the thes and, in fact, include every single word that this author wrote, you will probably later on go on your own turkey rampage.

I almost hate to tell you what will happen next. Edna and the sucky turkey story will zoom to the top of the Literature Hit Parade, and you will be reading it up to twenty-two times a day— ninety-seven times a day if you didn't have the foresight to get a job outside the home. Turkeys will start showing up in your dreams at night. Even more alarmingly, you and your husband will begin discussing the character development of the book, the plausibility of a duck being mistaken for a turkey by another turkey.

"Give me a break," you hear yourself saying. "A real turkey wouldn't have made that mistake even on the day she was hatched."

"But the point the author is making," says your husband, "is that self-esteem comes from self-acceptance— not trying to look like ducks when we're turkeys. It's Elbert I wonder about. What's his deal, strutting around like that?"

"I think he likes the fact that Edna admires him."

Then you both look at each other in horror. *What are we doing?*

One day it will occur to you that this turkey book could happen to get lost. Why not? Everything else in the house gets lost; why is this particular book the only object you can reliably lay your hands on, day after day, month after month? So you slip it under the couch cushions, or deep in the glove compartment of your car, or even toss it behind the clothes dryer, certain that you can put up with any crying and grief over the loss of this book far better than you can stand to read it again.

But there is no crying and grieving, because, through some sort of magic that only truly terrible books possess, it somehow beats you back into the kid's room. At last you see who you're dealing with. This turkey book is an adversary that cannot be vanquished. You have read it 4,578,974 times, and you realize you may have to read it another four and a half million times before your life can, blessedly, end. But just as you have resigned yourself to your fate—as you've perhaps realized you know the book so well that you can take a nap while you read it—its moment of fame abruptly ends, and it is sent by your child to the back of the closet, never to be heard from again.

The agony of a two-year-old decision-maker

There's nothing more heartrending than a two-year-old trying to decide between having her juice in the red cup or the green cup. This is a very dark chapter in human history, indeed, when mere babies have to make such momentous choices. Yet every single day that I was living with a toddler, I'd somehow forget that I was living with a person with a decision-making impairment, and I'd casually toss off a comment like, "Would you like to wear your blue shirt today or your yellow shirt?"

The next thing I knew, the kid would be in a screaming heap on the floor, doing her best impression of a nuclear meltdown, and I'd be wishing life came with a rewind button so I could undo the question.

"Okay, well, let's just go for the blue shirt," I'd say, trying to be helpful.

"NO! NOT THE BLUE SHIRT!"

"Ohhhhkayyyyyy. Then the yellow shirt."

"NO, NO, NO! I DON'T WANT THE YELLOW SHIRT! BLUE!"

"So then you want the blue?"

"I SAID NO BLUE! YELLOW SHIRT!"

"There are two shirts, yellow and blue. One of them is going on your body. Now which one will it be, the yellow or the blue?"

"Blue."

"Okay. We're putting on the blue."

"No. Yellow."

225

"All right. Are you sure? Yellow?"

"No. Blue."

"Are. You. Going. To. Wear. The. Blue. Shirt. Or. The. Yellow. Shirt?"

This, as near as I can tell, surely is the equivalent of asking a kid to decide between death by firing squad and death by jumping out of an airplane with no parachute. Eventually you realize that the kid is incapable of coming to such a decision, and that you are simply going to have to step in and enforce your own will, assuming you can work up an opinion yourself.

But, as you will discover, that was merely the first decision of the day. Other agonies await the two-year-old around every corner. Still to come are the land mines of which toys to play with, what to have for lunch, even whether to drink her milk or pour it on the floor.

If you possibly can manage it, you should try to leave home before lunchtime every day—or at least hire a babysitter and hide in the closet. I found that mealtimes were even worse for high-power decisions. After all, should the crust be cut off the bread or left on? Should it be peanut butter and jelly or peanut butter and cream cheese? Rectangles or triangles? Making a wrong decision on any of these questions can result in a sandwich needing to be thrown into the garbage can and a new sandwich started.

And then there are the incidental choices that come up every day: go to the store with Daddy, or stay home and torture Mommy? Rip out all the checks from the checkbook now, or wait until you've marked up the walls with purple marker? And come to think of it, why the purple marker? Maybe the red or black marker would be more effective. Throw shoes in the garbage can, or put them in the potty instead?

You'd like to help, you really would. But there's only one cure—and that's for the kid to turn thirty.

Chapter 16: What's So Great About the Potty?

The lies of toilet training

The three biggest lies in American society today are "The check's in the mail," "I'll still respect you in the morning," and "My kid was toilet trained by the time he was two."

Let's face it: Only certain toileting prodigies actually could be called toilet trained at this age; the rest of them are still regarding toilet water as something to bathe the cat in. And really now, be honest: If your child can only be a prodigy in one thing, wouldn't you really rather it be something besides peeing in a bowl?

The thing to remember about toilet training is that just about everybody on the planet does eventually get it. This fact is easy to forget when you're standing over an empty potty chair day after day, while diapers are filling up all around you. But frankly, toilet training seems to be yet another one of those things in life that the more you insist upon it, the less likely it is that it's going to happen—at least in your lifetime. For some metaphysical reason that probably only the Dalai Lama can explain, you have to stop caring about it before it can take place.

My friend Sue was of the determined school of toilet training, working diligently at it day after day all through babyhood and toddlerhood and, well, even starting to stray into what we would have to call the middle-kid years. This was especially tough on Sue because she hung out with a bunch of liars at the playground, all of whom claimed to have successfully toilet trained children at hysterically young ages. One woman was absolutely positive that she had once toilet trained a five-month-old. Technically speaking, of course.

"Now how could that be?" I said to Sue. "Unless this brilliant child was also able to walk himself to the potty chair."

"She says she would hold him over the potty chair at different times of the day, and he would go," said Sue.

"And all his diapers were dry?"

"That's what she says."

Now this, while an impressive feat, does not sound like true toilet training to me. It sounds neurotic, in fact. I'm seeing a fully grown woman willing to stand over the toilet bowl, hovering her baby in midair for what must have been hours on end, while she waited for stuff to emerge from him. Didn't she have any phone calls she needed to make?

Also—and I just wish the woman hadn't moved out of town before I thought of this—the whole story had to be a lie, because no one in her right mind would hold a baby boy in midair, waiting for him to pee. Baby boys, as we've all discovered at one time or another, pee straight up into the air, and his mother would have gotten a face full of you-know-what.

"So the whole thing's a lie," I said to Sue. "And this moving-out-of-town business—she probably was forced to go to a liar's colony or something. She's a danger to herself and society."

Oh, but she's far from the only toilet-training liar. At the playground where Sue took her (very damp) little boy, no one would admit to even ever seeing a child beyond the age of eighteen months who wasn't fully trained. Well, once, maybe there had been a two-year-old—but later it was discovered that he had, you know, other problems. Sue was miserable.

We were sitting in her kitchen, right next to the spotlessly gleaming potty chair. So far, she said, its bowl had only been used as a helmet, although once she thought she saw him eating cereal out of it as well.

"I had so hoped," she said, "to get him toilet trained before he left home. It just seems unfair that his wife should have to do this."

"Maybe it won't come to that," I said. "It could be his college will have a remedial toileting program."

Early efforts

All the books about toilet training—if you go in for that sort of reading matter—are clear about one thing: When you're intending to teach a child to use the potty, you pretty much have to take them along when you go to the toilet. This, the books say, is so they can see certain basics—for instance, that human beings are in no danger of falling in, and that the flushing noise, while dramatic, doesn't cause any undue damage.

All I can say is that you might as well take a wildcat with you to the bathroom. Before you have even gotten yourself fully lowered to the seat, your child, moving in a lightning-quick fashion, has managed to spin off most of the toilet paper from the roll, and it's now lying in accordion-type piles on the floor. Next, she's pulling towels off the towel racks and making costumes out of them. Then, before you can adjust yourself to grab her, she hides behind the shower curtain and starts twirling herself up in it while walking across the room. You leap up to steady it before the entire rod falls on her head.

"I a princess," she tells you.

"This," you say, "is the toilet paper. We use this for cleaning ourselves..."

But she doesn't hear you. Now she's climbing up onto the sink area to liberate the toothbrushes from their holders. You manage to jump up in time to save the bottle of hand lotion from spilling its contents into the sink, but the container of contact lens solution rolls over to the tub and the cap falls off.

"Toothbrushes want to go for a ride," she says. "This is the Mommy, this is the Daddy, this is the baby." She marches them around on the floor, through the contact lens solution, over to the toilet paper pile.

"I really don't like my toothbrush on the floor, and the toilet paper is supposed to stay on the roll," you say. "Put them back."

But she's found the toilet brush. "Ohhhh, a monster! Grrr! He will eat the Daddy and Mommy and baby. Oh, no! OH, NOOOOO!"

She rubs the toothbrushes into the bristles of the toilet brush, and you start screaming, too: "No! NO!"

Now the shower curtain rod really does fall, perhaps because the combined shrieks of the two of you have loosened some of the plaster. You pull yourself together and calmly manage to demonstrate the flushing of the toilet, just the way the books instructed you.

"You see? The toilet flush is just a water noise. Not scary at all."

She looks at you as though you're a very fragile being indeed to think the flushing could be the scary part. "The toilet brush is the monster," she says, tucking her hand into yours. "He eat up the toothbrushes."

Later, on your way to the store to buy new toothbrushes for the family as well as some plaster to reinstall the shower curtain rod and some contact lens solution, you realize you forgot to pee.

The fun things about the potty

It's not that young children have an aversion to using the toilet. It's just that they find the rest of us distinctly unimaginative when it comes to thinking up ways to use it. Eliminating into it is by far the most boring thing they can imagine, unless, of course, there's going to be a fishing expedition there later—a subject I don't even want to get into.

Besides doing their share of the family's washing responsibilities there—I knew one two-year-old who once was inspired to do the whole family's laundry in the commode—small children can be entertained for hours by standing beside it and throwing balls into it. You may not have realized that toilets are perfect as trainer basketball hoops for toddlers.

They are also useful as excellent storage spots for stuffed animals, particularly ones that your child perceives to be in need of cooling off. I came in once to find our household's population of teddy bears reclining in the toilet, and a child who earnestly explained to me that this was their pool.

"Teddy bears like the pool when they get hot," she said.

My friend Liz's son once decided to create an ecologically correct society in the toilet. She was pleased at how industriously he was working outside, loading up dirt and worms and leaves into his toy wheelbarrow—until later she found him ready to dump all this stuff into the toilet.

"What are you doing?" she shrieked.

"I making a lake. These are the trees."

It's this adventurous spirit that drives many of us to invest in potty chairs—those adorable little portable things that don't contain any water until the kid herself puts some in. Of course, potty chairs are also fun. Unlike the huge porcelain thing in the bathroom, they can be dragged everywhere, even worn on the head. Best of all, though, is that when certain impressive toileting events take place in them, there's no danger of them getting flushed away before all possible admirers have had a chance to view them.

The public potty—and other horrors

When you are training a kid to use the potty, you will become a virtual tour guide of Toilets of Your Town. Trust me: You will be on intimate terms with every scrungy hole of a public toilet as well as every never-meant-for-the-eyes-of-the-public toilet within a twenty-five-mile radius of your house.

This is because you reach a point where you will stop at nothing to get your kid to the bathroom in time. Nothing. No matter how many times you ask them, "Do you need to use the bathroom? Do you need to pee?" before you leave home, no matter how many times you even get them to squeeze a few drops out before you put them in their car seat, it is guaranteed that twenty minutes later, you'll hear, "MOMMY! Pee-pee, Mommy!"

This, in case you didn't know, is your three-second warning.

I have seen moms, upon hearing the three-second warning, jump out of moving vehicles and dangle small children over storm drains. I have seen them tuck kids under their arms, leap over barrels of nails in hardware stores, and mow down four customers, just so they can make it to the back of the store in time. And, worse, I have seen them pull portable potties out of their purses—their purses!—and set up a bathroom right in the middle of aisle three.

We do this because there's a hope among toilet trainers everywhere that if you can just get your child to stay dry for a twenty-four-hour period, then maybe the kid will get to hate the sensation of wet pants and will be motivated to use the toilet every time. You think that if you can just avoid the failure of even one setback, there is hope.

There is no greater hope than that experienced by parents who are trying to toilet train a kid.

But this, I'm afraid, is all a delusion. For every kid who discovers the joys of dry pants and converts to being a toilet-using person, there are ten kids who will look up at you from the sandbox, and with a straight face say, "I too busy to go potty. I can just wet my pants here." It's as though you had just brought him a platter of hors d'oeuvres when he'd really rather stick to his diet, thank you.

Still, this is why it's all the more meaningful when you hear the shriek of recognition that something is about to happen, bathroom-wise, and you know you have three seconds to get to the facilities, whatever they may be. This could be the Supreme Toileting Moment, the time when the whole idea will catch fire in his head and he'll never want to wear a diaper again. So you plead with garage mechanics, convenience store managers, and hot dog stand workers to pleeecease have mercy on a little child and let the two of you use their facilities.

Once in a convenience store, while my child did the Pee Dance, jumping all around and holding himself, the manager finally looked at me and said, "Wellll, it's not much, but I guess you can go back there, if you don't touch anything."

Later I realized he meant we shouldn't touch anything because unknown strains of bubonic plague and various blood diseases were growing rampant in cultures along every surface, and he was afraid we'd start a citywide epidemic.

Another time we were forced to take refuge in the postage stamp-sized, pitch-dark bathroom of a hardware store—more commonly known to the employees as the place to keep the extra rakes, push brooms, and snowblowers. The toilet itself was last used in 1967, the manager told me, which was also probably when the light bulb burned out. "That's when the McDonald's moved in across the street, and it just seemed easier to go over there when we had to go," he said.

"Yeah," I said. "That's great when you grow up and your bladder gives you more than a few seconds' warning."

After a few times of hazarding the life forms in public bathrooms, you may be tempted to get one of those potties that are meant for your purse, the kind you can just whip out at a moment's notice anywhere at all. Frankly, I don't think this is a direction you want to go in. If you're like most of us, it's likely that your purse already contains pacifiers, tissues, Lego pieces, baby doll arms, diapers, wipes, the wheels to two toy tractors, the H and the Z from the set of alphabet magnets, and the father from the dollhouse family. This in addition, of course, to your wallet, keys, sunglasses, receipt from the pediatrician's office, insurance form to be filled out then mailed, and a couple of rocks your kid liked at the playground yesterday. If you add a potty chair to this mix, I don't see how you're going to ever find anything again.

Besides which, when you're out in the world with a toddler, the main thing you need to be is agile. Toddlers can take off in a split second, and you're playing into their grimy little hands if you're weighted down with their freight and can't catch up to them.

Instead of hauling along your entire bathroom, invest in a good pair of running shoes—and maybe, just for safety's sake, some rubber gloves, a can of disinfectant, a roll of paper towels, and a light bulb. Then, I think, you'll be prepared for anything a public toilet has to offer you.

Waiting for poop

I don't know how to put this delicately, but when you have a child of a certain age, you're going to spend a great deal of your valuable, but dwindling, lifetime sitting on the floor of a bathroom somewhere, waiting for poop to come.

Pee is pretty cooperative about just coming out whenever it's beckoned, but, as one of my kids put it once, "Poops not so happy to leave." Sometimes you have to sit there for a hundred years or more, reading stories, chatting about current events, speculating about the long, slow process of colon peristalsis. Then, either an event finally occurs—or you black out. Either way, eventually you are allowed to leave and declare this chapter of your life done with, until later.

It helps if you had thought to install an entertainment center in your bathroom before you had a kid, but you probably didn't think of that in time. And now you must sit there, waiting and waiting, but what's worse is that you must be interesting while you wait. Unlike Waiting for Sleep when you're putting your child to bed—when you try to bore them to sleep—during Waiting for Poops, the kid needs constant distraction. She doesn't want to sit there any more than you do, and will constantly be getting up, hoisting up her clothing, and declaring that she'd just as soon poop in her pants—or never poop for the rest of her life, whatever she thinks will work with you.

Then you have to persuade her to sit back down and promise to do interesting things to while away the hours. Books, magazines, songs, even tap dances are good distractions. You'll find yourself telling jokes, doing impressions of all the Disney and Sesame Street characters, and speculating about what would happen if Winnie-the-Pooh would ever meet Barney. You can jitterbug, practice operatic arias, turn off the lights and play shadow games with the flashlight.

You can, in fact, do everything—except fall asleep or leave.

We had a book we read over and over again— thousands of times a week on the theory that it would put a certain little colon in the right mood. I knew that if by page 56—when the main character planted red tulips in his girlfriend's garden—we had not managed to plant something in the potty, that we were staring at Toileting Failure.

Next, we'd have to go in for the mind games: turning on the water, hoping that the psychological effect of flowing liquid might free up some of those brain cells that were obviously thinking, Hold back. Hold back.

Meditation and hypnosis were next, although hypnotizing a two-and-a-half-year-old has to be managed quickly and with great confidence. Mostly you say again and again, "I just know this is about to work. I can feel it getting close." You're like the Clipper of bathrooms.

Once, after a particularly long, unsatisfying afternoon around the potty chair, and after I'd exhausted my repertoire of dances, songs, impressions, and the final scene from Pagliacci, my daughter looked up at me and said, "I think the poop is packing his suitcase."

I wanted to bow down before it and shout, "Hallelujah!"

Chapter 17:
The Social Life of the Average American Toddler

These pals of mine

The time will come when your baby will start to acquire some friends. Luckily, for a while, you get to pick them out, based on how you get along with their mother. It's a case of, "Oh, Todd would be a nice boy for you to gum some rattles with, because his mom and I both work in the marketing department, and besides that, we both drink tea instead of coffee and we go to the same place to get our hair cut." Later—say around adolescence—this system won't work so much, so you should enjoy it while you're the chief friend picker.

These little get-togethers are very enlightening, mostly because you get to hear that other women also have sixteen pacifiers in various, unknown locations throughout their houses and cars, and that they, too, have babies who ate their tax return and some toenail clippings that were left on the coffee table by mistake. You can bond very easily over disclosures like that.

But the best part is that if you get together on a regular basis with other mothers and their children (this, I think, is technically called a play group), you get to see everybody's baby turn from a little lump of primitive human protoplasm into a little person with a real personality. Mostly this is a good thing, although it will introduce you to a new facet of your personality: the part that's capable of being consumed with helpless rage at somebody else's eighteen-month-old, simply because that kid is ignoring your kid. Believe me, there will be times you just wish you could ask some other little toddler to step outside with you, so the two of you could get a few things straight.

Also, toddlers are very hilarious to watch. As they emerge from their adorable baby blob state, they start to take on real personalities. Even when they're still technically babies, you can see them playing roles within the play group and working out basic human issues, like who has the best pacifier.

The good thing to remember when you hang out with two- and three-year-olds is that they're totally irrational beings—and that nothing that happens now is forever. They are all peculiar in their own way.

Here are some of the roles they play when they all get together.

The CEO: Because every group—even a group of people in diapers—has to have a leader, one will appear in your child's play group, too. Chances are, it's going to turn out to be the kid who can say the word "Mine!" with the most ringing authority, or who has some other adult attribute that other kids can't help but respect. At my daughter's play group, there was a two-year-old there who, through some kind of genetic anomaly, had skipped the Baby Hair Stage and gone directly to adult hair. It hung down her back in a long, brown ponytail, at an age when all the rest of the two-year-olds still had managed only to grow a couple of wisps here and there. Believe me, we all—mothers and kids alike—looked up to her and respected her views because of this. One day I found myself asking her advice on whether I should get my own hair cut. Whenever her mother would tell stories about her—stories that made her sound like a regular two-year-old with tantrums and pacifier issues—I couldn't believe we were talking about the same person. I mean, this kid seemed so together that I could easily picture her in a business suit with a briefcase, running an entire corporation. At the very least, I thought she should have her own apartment and the keys to the car.

The Biter: When this kid's around, you can practically hear the theme from *Jaws* start to play in the background. He's the one who has suddenly figured out that those painful things that sprouted some time ago in his gums actually have a use: They are objects of terror. It's a temporary stage, to be sure, but for a while, all this kid has to do is to bare his teeth menacingly, and all the mothers rush to throw their bodies over their own dear children.

Biting is such an effective means to ending a dispute for babies that nearly all of them try it at some point, but when it's your kid doing the biting, you will feel like scum. You will be stricken with shame that you have failed to better educate your child against resorting to violence.

"But when was I supposed to get this across to her?" wailed my friend Kathy one day, when her adorable little daughter had taken out three playmates in the sandbox one morning. "She only just started speaking English two weeks ago!"

It's good if you can manage to be nice to the mother who's child is currently doing the chewing on other kids—that way, when it's your kid biting, everybody may still be nice to you.

The Escape Artist: This kid isn't made of bones and muscles like regular human beings. Instead he's composed of some kind of wiry substance—most likely the materials that suspend bungee jumpers from cranes. Not only that, but for some reason, he's learned early to perform feats of athletic prowess that only

Hollywood stuntmen know about. At eight months, his mother will tell you, he was crawling across the tops of

239

the kitchen cabinets in search of glass objects he could hurl to the floor. Now that he's in the toddler stage, he tries to disappear whenever you look the other way even for ten seconds. And he has every possible physical advantage, including the ability to roll himself into a ball the size of dryer lint when you're looking for him. The other odd thing about him is that when you do grab him as he runs past, it actually hurts your hand to touch him. It's like trying to latch onto a piece of steel that's flying past.

The Slimy One: How to put this? Some children just seem to excel in secretions. Their particular talent seems to be oozing shiny gelatinous substances from every orifice: drool, mucus, eye water—possibly even earwax. You find yourself fantasizing about bringing in a big hose and turning it on the kid, full blast, just to see if you can blow off the top layer at least. The mother seems as perplexed by this as anyone, since she seems to be a perfectly dry person herself. She'll go to pick him up and he'll slip out of her grip. "Nobody ever told me that children are so slippery," she'll say.

The Clingy One: When this child belongs to you, life in the play group is like a hell on earth. This kid doesn't want to stray even one inch from Mama. In fact, her expression is so serious all the time that you can just tell she's doing the mathematical calculations to determine if she could still fit in the womb. Whenever others speak to her, she looks at them with shock, as though she's seen their pictures on the wanted posters at the post office. She won't even go near the other kids until a suitable warm-up period has taken place—maybe six years or so.

But there are miracles in the play group. One day, the biter stops using his teeth to make his point, and instead of displaying his gleaming white weapons, he simply asks the kid next to him for the Batman action figure. The slimy one dries up, the clinger ventures forth into the sandbox and makes a pancake out of dirt, and the escape artist

240

concentrates on climbing to the top of the sliding board and scaring his mother by standing on one foot thirty feet above her head.

They are bonding. And you realize you like the other mothers, even though they aren't people you ever would have met otherwise.

Toddler love

You probably thought you wouldn't have to deal with your child's love life until junior high or so. But, frankly, you're lucky if your kid waits until toddlerhood for her first major affair. When babies fall in love, the results can be devastating. It almost always ends badly.

My youngest child fell for an older man of two when she was still just seventeen months. I told her this was a mistake. "You're still measuring your lifetime in months, while he's moved on to years," I pointed out. "I think this quite literally qualifies as a May-December romance."

You could just see this romance was doomed. For one thing, he'd been around the block a few times, and knew many more words than she did. Even though he was patient, she had trouble keeping up with his wild ways. For instance, he liked yelling "La! La! La!" into mail slots at their babysitter's apartment, and she couldn't pronounce Ls correctly, so she had to say "Ya! Ya! Ya!" which really isn't the same thing at all. You could see him frowning whenever she'd say it.

Things were going along okay, though, until he brought another girl—his next-door neighbor—to the babysitter's house one day. Even when you're seventeen months old, you know your relationship is in trouble when he's parading your replacement right in front of you.

The new girl was obviously a bombshell. She had curly blond hair. (My daughter was still sporting her Dwight Eisenhower look.) She was wearing a dress with frills and flowers. (My daughter until then only wanted to wear her OshKosh overalls, the ones with the holes in the knees.) And get this—she had black patent leather shoes and socks with lace on the cuffs.

Let me tell you: The pain was palpable.

The babysitter said it got bad at lunchtime, when both girls tried to save a seat at the lunch table for The Guy. When he chose to sit in the chair that the bombshell had saved for him, my poor daughter stomped over and tried to drag him over to her seat. But worse was when it came time to yell into the mail slots, and the bombshell ran ahead and did all the yelling first, pronouncing each L with precision. At that point, my daughter just sat down on the sidewalk and burst into tears.

I, of course, wanted to throttle this two-year-old girl. I was ready to call her mother and insist that she be grounded for the next five years. "And what do you mean," I would say, "letting your daughter wear those socks with the lace on the cuffs? Next, I suppose, you'll be giving her fishnet stockings and halter tops!" But the babysitter was giving me quizzical looks, so I tried to smile and simply strap my weeping child into her car seat. It's best to leave with your dignity intact in these circumstances, if at all possible.

On the way home, I tried my best Romantic Tragedy Speeches—you know, "There's other fish in the sea" and "He wasn't any good anyway. Better that you know now than after you've put in any more time into this relationship."

Later, I talked to my husband about whether or not we should look around for another babysitter.

"Are you serious?" he said. "Miranda is a great baby sitter."

"But think of your daughter! To be at the scene of her heartbreak every day might just get to be too much," I said. "These are such delicate, tender feelings, you know. This could affect her whole life. This could determine whether or not we ever get any grandchildren!"

He stared. "You know, you're really beginning to scare me."

Fortunately, though, we didn't have to take any action. The bombshell's parents decided not to send her to the babysitter every day after all. Possibly they were scared off by our little Kojak, or maybe they found a finishing school she could attend, I don't really know. Soon after, our kid learned to say "La! La! La!" and grew some hair, and by then she didn't seem so interested in romance anymore. When you're a toddler, the fact that you have the attention span of a gnat really can work in your favor.

The birthday party scene

There is one thing to remember when you're throwing your child a birthday party: Don't let it be at your house.

In fact, if you can somehow keep yourself from giving a party at all, that would probably be the sanest choice. But for some reason, that never seems to be an option. Your relatives, at the very least, are going to want to come over and eat birthday cake and ice cream with the child. And then, how's it going to look if they get there and your child has no friends to celebrate with? They're going to think you're raising one of those people who'll eventually head for the wilderness, brandish shotguns, and write treatises against society.

Besides, you have to admit that there is just the tiniest part of you that wants to have the whole birthday bonanza: balloons, clowns, a dozen squealing toddlers spilling punch on the rug. You don't know why, but for weeks, you are irresistibly drawn to mailing out party invitations and calling on birthday entertainers. This is what parenthood is all about, right?

Okay, if you can't stop yourself, then just take my advice and don't let any clowns attend. For some reason that only small children know, clowns are the scariest people in the whole world. I have gone to birthday parties where the only person in sight was the clown, performing his act all alone. Everybody else was hiding behind the couch, or else had crawled underneath the kitchen sink, wailing. Even the moms were quaking a little. Finally, the birthday child's mother climbed out from her hiding place and begged the clown to take his big shoes, his funny red nose, his money, and get the hell out before mental health authorities were going to be required.

Don't go into this birthday party business blindly, as I have done. It's best if you know in advance that the main activity, no matter what you've planned, is going to be hitting. Spilling juice is also very popular, as are crying and grabbing all the birthday presents away before the birthday person can open them. This is a very important activity at a two-year-old's birthday party. Any guest who doesn't put up a fight when it comes time to leave her present with the birthday kid is simply not doing her job and is probably coming down with something.

Your own child—the guest of honor—is required by statute to have at least two major temper tantrums and several minor skirmishes, which all your relatives (the kindly ones, anyway) will explain as "too much excitement." At the point when your kid starts knocking fellow toddlers over the head with the boxes from the presents, your kindly relatives will smile and say, "Too much sugar." You don't want to think about what the not-so-kind relatives are giving as causes, but believe me, your breast-feeding habits have been mentioned.

My friend Jane, a brave woman, once decided to give her two-year-old son a pudding party. She made up vats of vanilla and chocolate pudding, set them in gigantic plastic mixing bowls outside, and placed the guests all around them with wooden spoons. In no time, everyone was undressed and beating his neighbor over the head with a spoon. And after the adults broke up the fights, treated the injured, and tried to avoid being slimed with pudding ourselves, we all ended up admitting that this would be a great idea for a grown-up's

244

party. Then we got the hoses and watched as Jane's roses were fertilized with dairy products.

This kind of at-home torture is why it may be best to go to one of those public institutions that specializes in birthday parties. It's true, you have to pay a fortune, and they sometimes have some rather terrifying dancing animal puppets, and the voice of your Birthday Party Handler may cause you to develop a facial tic, but all in all, I think you come out ahead. At least when the pizza and birthday cake are flying around the room, you know none of it is going to land on your own personal carpet.

And eventually—although it may not seem so—you get to go home.

Advice About Birthday Parties

- Never ever let a child know the exact date of his birthday. That way, you can hold the party whenever it's convenient. There's an eleven-month statute of limitations on this, however; otherwise, you have to give two birthday parties simultaneously.
- Don't give a birthday party that conflicts with naptime, mealtime, or bedtime. This means that for the first birthday, there's approximately a fifteen-minute interval in which the party could take place, so don't let the guests get too comfortable. You might want to serve the birthday cake in take-out boxes.
- As horrible as clowns are, ponies may be even worse.
- Hide the birthday presents once they're opened, or every single kid is going to try to take his own present back home with him. I've seen major meltdowns, when all the kids and most of the adults are in a rage by the end of the party.
- Nobody under thirty likes a birthday hat with an elastic band under the chin.

- Make sure the birthday kid doesn't eat the presents before they get opened. Bright wrapping paper looks mighty delicious.
- Two words: plastic mats. Put them underneath everything.
- Chocolate icing is a bad idea.
- Whatever your drug of choice to get through the day—aspirin, beer, straight-up martinis—I think you really have to let all the other parents have some too.

Chapter 18: Things You Could Feel Guilty About

- One day you forgot to set the parking brake on the stroller, and it rolled about two feet before you noticed—and what if it had rolled in the other direction and gone into traffic?
- You told your husband that the obstetrician had said no sex for six months, when really it was closer to six minutes.
- You haven't done even one sit-up since the baby was born.
- Someone asked you if you had children, and you said, "No—wait, I mean yes!"
- Sometimes you wish the baby didn't look like Uncle Fester quite so much.
- You have never bolted the car seat to the frame of the car.
- So far, despite trying to economize, you have spent $56.78 on pacifiers because you keep losing them.
- Instead of reading Mother Goose or Winnie-the-Pooh, you read a trashy novel to your six-month-old, because you had to know how it ended, and besides, how would she ever know the difference?
- You really should have stuck with piano lessons back in seventh grade because now you have no sense of self-discipline to pass on to your child.

- You don't change poopy diapers if you hear your husband's car in the driveway. You save them for him to discover when he says hello to the baby.
- You really did go ahead and buy the baby tuxedo, size 3-6 months.
- Nobody has yet gotten any baby pictures from you—and some of your relatives even think the baby's birth was a month later, simply because you didn't get around to notifying people for four weeks.
- You ate a whole cheesecake by yourself and then threw away the evidence in somebody else's trash can.
- You sat, mesmerized, by the baby monitor, listening to a gossipy conversation about people you know—and when the baby woke up from her nap and started crying, you brought her in to listen too.
- After spending a day with a feverish, sickly baby who threw up five times, you now know for sure that you have no patience.
- You feel that Baby Hair Washing should be an Olympic event, and since you're not the athletic type, you do it as little as possible—mainly when food gets in the hair.
- You have told so many people that you only gained fifteen pounds during your pregnancy that now you believe it yourself.

Chapter 19: Romantic Evening

No one knows for sure how this happens.

You wake up in the middle of the night, hearing the heater making a funny noise. Next to you, your husband is sleeping— one arm thrust out across the pillow, mouth open, a little fleck of drool just starting to make its way to the whiskers on his cheek.

Outside, it's raining, and you remember that you left the car windows down, and that the tricycle is outside. Earlier today, the dog threw up on the rug, thirteen telemarketers called during dinner, and you discovered your Macy's bill didn't get paid because it had been stuffed into the Little Tykes coffcepot, along with some mud and water. Your child said it was being dipped in coffee to make it taste better.

You get out of bed and tiptoe down the hall to find out why the kid is sleeping in his own bed for the first time since anyone can remember. Maybe you'll have to take a pulse.

But no, there he is -sleeping on his stomach with his butt up in the air, his legs curled under him in those little footed pajamas. His thumb has just fallen out of his mouth, and there are approximately seven pacifiers visible from where you are standing.

On the way back to bed, you trip over a riding toy, a couple of Matchbox cars, and a life-sized stuffed elephant. You barely keep from cursing. When you get back to bed, with your toe throbbing, your husband turns and smiles in his sleep as he reaches for you.

"I think it's time," you say to him, "for another one."

Later, someone might ask you just how it was you knew it was time for number two. And the only thing you know for sure is that life's a mess and is probably going to stay that way, but your pre-pregnancy jeans fit again, and you and your husband have the bed to yourself.

And you figure that if you can do it once, you can certainly do it again.

CHAPTER ONE

NINA

The morning after my mother's funeral, before I had changed the sheets on her bed, before I even knew if I was going to survive living without her, I went into the kitchen and took the fifteen unlabeled casserole dishes from the refrigerator and, one by one, scooped out their moldy contents and hurled all that food out the back door into the snow.

It was the happiest I'd felt in weeks. No, months.

Well-meaning people had brought these as an offering of kindness. People I loved who thought that not bringing food to the dying was maybe the worst thing you could ever do—and I had been grateful. But we couldn't keep up, my mother and I. The casserole dishes stacked up like accusations in the refrigerator. When I opened the door, they shouted their grievances.

I stood there watching as pieces of macaroni, ham, lima beans, squash, and unidentified red items went flying against the deep-blue February sky, then landed on the snowbank, where they created an instant abstract painting. One spunky little yellow casserole dish escaped my hands and bounced off the railing of the porch and then crashed across the ice, and smashed into a million pieces near the garbage cans.

I gave that one a standing ovation, then got my phone and took a picture of the hillside canvas, now splattered with reds and beiges and greens.

I messaged it to Dan, my ex, with one sentence: *When someone dies, people bring horrifying food and I make art of it,* and he wrote back immediately: *You know Julie doesn't like it when you text me first thing in the a.m.*

Tough, I typed. *She shoulda thought of that when she started dating a married man.* He wrote: *WE ARE NOT MARRIED, NINA.* And then I wrote: *But we WERE* and clicked off the phone so I didn't have to hear from Julie about how I was being inappropriate and could I please respect the boundaries she and Dan were trying to set. Last week she actually wrote, *We are being patient because we know your mom is dying but please respect our space.*

I walked through the silent townhouse—silent, that is, except for the sounds of voices in the units on either side. Normal people all getting ready for their next normal day, not even thinking about how lucky they were to be alive.

It was seven twenty-two, the time of the day my mom and I used to have our first healthy shake of the day. We'd lie on her rented hospital bed next to the picture window and watch Kathie Lee and Hoda until some serious topic came up, which would then make my mother remember that we weren't laughing enough. She had decided to treat her stage-four liver cancer with laughter and green smoothies. The drowsy days had flowed into one another, one Mel Brooks movie after another, none distinguishable from the next. We were on Cancer Time now, she said.

Toward the end, she stopped being her regular self and started saying things she felt like talking about, even stuff I suspected she'd never wanted me to know. It was as though the filters had come off. For instance, she'd had sex before she got married. She told me it had happened in a man's car, on a hilltop, and it had been awkward as hell but the worst part had been that her underpants had somehow gotten lost under the front seat and it was dark so she'd had to go home without them, and the man returned them to her at work the next day in a brown paper bag—the kind you'd pack a school lunch in.

"Who would do such a thing?" she said. "Wouldn't a gentleman know to simply politely dispose of them and pretend he'd never seen them?"

"Wow," I said. "You're still carrying that?"

And she said, "Well, now it's become a funny story. I was waiting for that to happen."

Also, she told me, she'd always loved my father but, well, he'd been a bit of a stick sometimes, and there were two full years after the infertility treatments when she really thought she might have left him if they hadn't adopted me by then. And other things came up, too: she'd always meant to go to Austria and play the piano and wear stilettos. She hadn't ever been to the tropics. As a child, she wanted to raise chimpanzees. Silly dreams, she called them. She hoped I hadn't minded too much that I was the only child they'd had, that I hadn't been too lonely with just the two of them. I'd always known I was adopted, that they cherished me in a special way because they'd worked so hard to find me— "looked the whole world over," as my mother had put it when I was a child. But I had known enough not to ask too many questions; I knew, the way a child knows these things, that it would crush my mother if I asked where I had come from, who I really belonged to.

And then late one night came the big one: "If you want to know who you really are, if you want to find your real mother, there's a nun at the Connecticut Catholic Children's Agency who will help you," she said. "Sister Germaine, that's her name. In New Ashbury. That's where the orphanage is."

The world inside my head started spinning out, slowly. The orphanage was two towns over. I'd never known.

"Funny," she said softly, so softly I could barely hear her, "funny that you never asked. Your dad and I were a little surprised, frankly, at your lack of curiosity. He said it must be because you were happy with us. That you didn't need anyone else."

Later, after I thought she was long asleep, she said in a drowsy voice, "Oh, and there's a photograph somewhere. I can't remember where I put it, but you'll find it when you clean everything out, I suppose."

"A photograph? Of what?" I said. My heart sat upright in the bed.

"I don't know. Of you, I guess, and your birth mother. The adoption agency gave it to me the day they gave you to me." She made a clicking sound. "All that worry, all those years, about your real mother showing up. And for no reason. And now . . . well, we're safe."

Safe, I thought, was a funny word to use when every cell in your body has gone all malignant on you, and you're hours from death. But maybe safe is just a matter of perspective.

***

I, however, knew I was not safe. She died three days later with her faith intact and her conscience clear, knowing exactly where she was headed, but I needed a road map back to a life without her. Fueled by my stunning success with the casserole dishes, I sat on the kitchen floor and made a to-do list.

NINA POPKIN'S POST-APOCALYPTIC PLAN FOR REGULAR LIFE:

Return Mel Brooks movies to Netflix. Suggest they put a warning on them that they are useless—useless!—against cancer.

Call the hospital bed rental place and tell them to get this stupid bed of death out of the living room!!!! Then move the couch and end tables and normal people furniture back in from the dining room.

Take the portable commode, the shower chair, and the IV pole to the recycling place.

Do the following in one very busy, probably very bad day: Call Mom's attorney, put medical bills in one pile, open insurance statements, clean out the attic, burn all your school papers she saved through the years (BUT BE CAREFUL not to burn the photo of you and your real mom, if it even exists), put condo on the market, sell all the furniture, move someplace fabulous.

Take deep breaths. You did the best you could. You can't cure cancer.

Stop texting Dan.

Long-term: Go on a cruise to Barbados, take dancing lessons, buy a farm in Vermont, sign up for a space mission to Mars, open a bar, learn to make baked Alaska, take voice lessons, ice-skate at midnight, French braid your hair, fall in love with somebody wonderful.

Stop crying.

A few hours later, I added:

Find your real mom, find your real mom, find your real mom, find your real mom.

Discover More

Nonfiction

Sleeping Through the Night…and Other Lies

You Might As Well Laugh: Surviving the Joys of Parenthood

Even June Cleaver Would Forget the Juice Box: Cut Yourself Some Slack (and Still Raise Great Kids) in the Age of Extreme Parenting

Fiction

A Piece of Normal

What Comes After Crazy

Kissing Games of the World

The Stuff that Never Happened

The Survivor's Guide to Family Happiness

About the Author

I was born in Jacksonville, Florida, where I wrote my first book of fiction (a story about a king who was tired) when I was five years old and sold it to the neighbors so I could get money for ice cream. Since then, I've been a newspaper reporter, a columnist for *Working Mother* magazine, a freelance writer, the author of three non-fiction humor books about parenting—and now, at last, as the author of several novels, writing as Maddie Dawson.

http://www.maddiedawson.com/

CPSIA information can be obtained
at www.ICGtesting.com
Printed in the USA
LVHW03s1518280818
588394LV00010B/806/P